The Unemployed Fortune-Teller

POETS ON POETRY · Donald Hall, General Editor

DONALD HALL *Goatfoot Milktongue Twinbird · The Weather for Poetry ·*
Poetry and Ambition · Death to the Death of Poetry
GALWAY KINNELL *Walking Down the Stairs*
WILLIAM STAFFORD *Writing the Australian Crawl · You Must Revise Your Life*
DONALD DAVIE *Trying to Explain*
MAXINE KUMIN *To Make a Prairie*
DIANE WAKOSKI *Toward a New Poetry*
ROBERT BLY *Talking All Morning*
ROBERT FRANCIS *Pot Shots at Poetry*
DAVID IGNATOW *Open Between Us*
RICHARD KOSTELANETZ *The Old Poetries and the New*
LOUIS SIMPSON *A Company of Poets · The Character of the Poet · Ships Going into the Blue*
PHILIP LEVINE *Don't Ask*
JOHN HAINES *Living Off the Country*
MARGE PIERCY *Parti-Colored Blocks for a Quilt*
JAMES WRIGHT *Collected Prose*
MARVIN BELL *Old Snow Just Melting*
ALICIA OSTRIKER *Writing Like a Woman*
JOHN LOGAN *A Ballet for the Ear*
HAYDEN CARRUTH *Effluences from the Sacred Caves · Suicides and Jazzers*
ROBERT HAYDEN *Collected Prose*
DONALD JUSTICE *Platonic Scripts*
JOHN FREDERICK NIMS *A Local Habitation*
ANNE SEXTON *No Evil Star*
CHARLES SIMIC *The Uncertain Certainty · Wonderful Words, Silent Truth ·*
The Unemployed Fortune-Teller
TESS GALLAGHER *A Concert of Tenses*
WELDON KEES *Reviews and Essays, 1936–55*
CHARLES WRIGHT *Halflife*
WILLIAM MATTHEWS *Curiosities*
TOM CLARK *The Poetry Beat*
WILLIAM MEREDITH *Poems Are Hard to Read*
PETER DAVISON *One of the Dangerous Trades*
AMY CLAMPITT *Predecessors, Et Cetera*
JANE MILLER *Working Time*
DAVID LEHMAN *The Line Forms Here · The Big Question*
DANIEL HOFFMAN *Words to Create a World*
GREGORY ORR *Richer Entanglements*
FRED CHAPPELL *Plow Naked*
ROBERT CREELEY *Tales Out of School*
THOM GUNN *Shelf Life*
MARY KINZIE *The Judge Is Fury*
ALAN WILLIAMSON *Eloquence and Mere Life*
MARIANNE BORUCH *Poetry's Old Air*

Charles Simic

The Unemployed
Fortune-Teller

ESSAYS AND MEMOIRS

Ann Arbor
THE UNIVERSITY OF MICHIGAN PRESS

1997   1996   1995   4   3   2

A CIP catalogue record for this book is available from the British Library.

Library of Congress Cataloging-in-Publication Data

Simic, Charles, 1938–
    The unemployed fortune-teller : essays and memoirs /
Charles Simic.
        p.   cm. — (Poets on poetry)
    Includes bibliographical references.
    ISBN 0-472-09569-2 (alk. paper). — ISBN 0-472-06569-6
(pbk. : alk. paper)
    1. Simic, Charles, 1938– . 2. Poets, American—20th
century—Biography. 3. Poetics. 4. Poetry. I. Title.
II. Series.
PS3569.I472Z473   1994
811'.54—dc20   94-16088
                                                    CIP

for Philip

Acknowledgments

Grateful acknowledgment is made to the following journals and publishers for permission to reprint previously published material:

Antaeus for "Don't Squeeze the Tomatoes!," Spring 1994; "Food and Happiness," Spring 1992; and "No Cure for the Blues," Fall 1993.

Aperture for "Shop, Le Bacarès" in *Paul Strand: Essays on His Life and Work.* Copyright © 1990.

Boulevard for "Lady Be Good," Fall 1993; 70–77.

The Drawing Center for "The Little Venus of the Eskimos."

Field for introduction to *Night Mail, Selected Poems of Novica Tadić.* Copyright © 1992.

Gettysburg Review for "Luneville Diary," Fall 1993.

Menard Press for the preface to *Red Knight.* Copyright © 1992.

The New Republic for "Elegy in a Spider's Web."

Ohio Review for "Fried Sausage," Fall 1992.

Scribners for an introduction to *The Best American Poetry 1992.* Copyright © 1993.

Western Humanities Review for "Poetry Is the Present," Spring 1991.

Every effort has been made to trace the ownership of copyrighted material in this book and to obtain permission for its use.

Contents

The Flute Player in the Pit   1

Food and Happiness   6

The Little Venus of the Eskimos   13

Fried Sausage   19

Bicycle Thieves   22

Lady Be Good   26

Elegy in a Spider's Web   34

Novica Tadić   40

Shop, Le Bacarès   43

No Cure for the Blues   46

Poetry Is the Present   53

The Necessity of Poetry   58

Luneville Diary   75

Red Knight   98

The Minotaur Loves His Labyrinth   101

Sigmund Abeles   115

Aleš Debeljak   118

Don't Squeeze the Tomatoes!   120

The Flute Player in the Pit

I say the word or two that has to be said . . . and remind every
man and every woman of something.

—Walt Whitman

Thirty years ago in New York City I used to stay up late almost
every night listening to Jean Shepherd's rambling soliloquies
on the radio. He had a show with a lot of interesting talk and a
little music. One night he told a lengthy story, which I still
remember, about the sacred ritual of some Amazon tribe. It
went roughly like this:

Once every seven years, the members of this remote tribe
would dig a deep hole in the jungle and lower their finest
flute player into it. He would be given no food, only a little
water and no way of climbing out. After this was done, the
other members of the tribe would bid him good-bye, never to
return. Seven days later, the flute player, sitting crosslegged at
the bottom of his hole, would begin to play. Of course, the
tribesmen could not hear him, only the gods could, and that
was the point.

According to Shepherd, who was not above putting on his
audience of insomniacs, an anthropologist had hidden him-
self during the ritual and recorded the man playing the flute.
Tonight Shepherd was going to play that very tape.

I was spooked. Here was a man, soon to die, already dizzy
with hunger and despair, summoning whatever strength and
belief in gods he had. A New World Orpheus, it occurred to me.

Shepherd went on talking until finally, in the wee-hour
silence of the night and my shabby room on East 13th Street,
the faint sound of the otherworldly flute was heard: its soli-

---

Written as an introduction to *The Best American Poetry 1992*.

tary, infinitely sad squeak with the raspy breath of the living human being still audible in it from time to time, making the best of his predicament. I didn't care then nor do I care now whether Shepherd made up the whole story. We are all at the bottom of our own private pits, even here in New York.

All the arts are about the impossible predicament. That's their fatal attraction. "Words fail me," poets often say. Every poem is an act of desperation or, if you prefer, a throw of the dice. God is the ideal audience, especially if you can't sleep or if you're in a hole in the Amazon. If he's absent, so much the worse.

The poet sits before a blank piece of paper with a need to say many things in the small space of the poem. The world is huge, the poet is alone, and the poem is just a bit of language, a few scratchings of a pen surrounded by the silence of the night.

It could be that the poet wishes to tell you about his or her life. A few images of some fleeting moment when one was happy or exceptionally lucid. The secret wish of poetry is to stop time. The poet wants to retrieve a face, a mood, a cloud in the sky, a tree in the wind, and take a kind of mental photograph of that moment in which you as a reader recognize yourself. Poems are other people's snapshots in which we recognize ourselves.

Next, the poet is driven by the desire to tell the truth. "How is truth to be said?" asks Gwendolyn Brooks. Truth matters. Getting it right matters. The realists advise: open your eyes and look. People of imagination warn: close your eyes to see better. There's truth with eyes open and there's truth with eyes closed and they often do not recognize each other on the street.

Next, one wishes to say something about the age in which one lives. Every age has its injustices and immense sufferings, and ours is scarcely an exception. There's the history of human vileness to contend with and there are fresh instances every day to think about. One can think about it all one wants, but making sense of it is another matter. We live in a time in which there are hundreds of ways of explaining the world. Everything from every variety of religion to every species of scientism is believed. The task of poetry, perhaps, is to salvage a trace of the authentic from the wreckage of religious, philosophical, and political systems.

Next, one wants to write a poem so well crafted that it would do honor to the tradition of Emily Dickinson, Ezra Pound, and Wallace Stevens, to name only a few masters.

At the same time, one hopes to rewrite that tradition, subvert it, turn it upside down and make some living space for oneself.

At the same time, one wants to entertain the reader with outrageous metaphors, flights of imagination, and heartbreaking pronouncements.

At the same time, one has, for the most part, no idea of what one is doing. Words make love on the page like flies in the summer heat and the poet is merely the bemused spectator. The poem is as much the result of chance as of intention. Probably more so.

At the same time, one hopes to be read and loved in China in a thousand years the same way the ancient Chinese poets are loved and read in our own day, and so forth.

This is a small order from a large menu requiring one of those many-armed Indian divinities to serve as a waiter.

One great defect of poetry, or one of its sublime attractions—depending on your view—is that it wants to include everything. In the cold light of reason, poetry is impossible to write.

Of course, there would be no anthology of best poems if the impossible did not happen occasionally. Authentic poems get written, and that's the best-kept secret in any age. In the history of the world the poet is ever present, invisible and often inaudible. Just when everything else seems to be going to hell in America, poetry is doing fine. The predictions of its demise, about which we so often read, are plain wrong, just as most of the intellectual prophecies in our century have been wrong. Poetry proves again and again that any single overall theory of anything doesn't work. Poetry is always the cat concert under the window of the room in which the official version of reality is being written. The academic critics write, for instance, that poetry is the instrument of the ideology of the ruling class and that everything is political. The tormentors of Anna Akhmatova are their patron saints. But what if poets are not crazy? What if they convey the feel of a historical period better than anybody else? Obviously, poetry engages something essential and overlooked in human beings, and it is this ineffable quality that has always ensured its longevity. "To glimpse the essential . . . stay flat on your back all day, and moan," says E. M. Cioran. There's more than that to poetry, of course, but that's a beginning.

Lyric poets perpetuate the oldest values on earth. They assert the individual's experience against that of the tribe. Emerson claimed that to be a genius meant "to believe your own thoughts, to believe that what is true for you in your private heart is true for all men." Lyric poetry since the Greeks has always assumed something like that, but American poetry since Whitman and Emerson has made it its main conviction. Everything in the world, profane or sacred, needs to be reexamined repeatedly in the light of one's own experience.

Here, now, I, amazed to find myself living my life . . . The American poet is a modern citizen of a democracy who lacks any clear historical, religious, or philosophical foundation. Sneering Marxists used to characterize such statements as "typical bourgeois individualism." "They adore the smell of their own shit," a fellow I used to know said about poets. He was a Maoist, and the idea of each human being finding his or her own truth was incomprehensible to him. Still, this is what Robert Frost, Charles Olson, and even Elizabeth Bishop had in mind. They were realists who had not yet decided what reality is. Their poetry defends the sanctity of that pursuit in which reality and identity are forever being rediscovered.

It's not imagination or ideas that our poets primarily trust, but examples, narratives, or specific experiences. There's more than a little of the Puritan diarist still left in poets. Like their ancestors, they worry about the state of their inner lives in between entries about the weather. The problem of identity is ever present, as is the nagging suspicion that one's existence lacks meaning. The working premise, nevertheless, is that each self, even in its most private concerns, is representative, that the "aesthetic problem," as John Ashbery has said, is a "microcosm of all human problems," that the poem is a place where the "I" of the poet, by a kind of visionary alchemy, becomes a mirror for all of us.

"America is not finished, perhaps never will be," Whitman said. Our poetry is the dramatic knowledge of that state. Its heresy is that it takes a part of the truth for the whole truth and makes it a "temporary stay against confusion," in Robert Frost's famous formulation. In physics it is the infinitely small that contradicts the general law, and the same is true of poetry at its best. What we love in it is its democracy of values, its recklessness, its individualism, and its freedom. There's nothing more American and more hopeful than its poetry.

one dark, still Sunday
—H. D. Thoreau

The black dog on the chain wags his tail as I walk by. The house and the barn of his master are sagging, as if about to collapse with the weight of the sky. On my neighbor's porch and in his yard there are old cars, stoves, refrigerators, washing machines, and dryers that he keeps carting back from the town dump for some unclear and still undecided future use. All of it is broken, rusty, partly dismantled and scattered about, except for the new-looking and incongruous plaster statue of the Virgin with eyes lowered as if embarrassed to be there. Past his house, there's a spectacular winter sunset over the lake, the kind one used to see in paintings sold in back of discount department stores. As for the flute player, I remember reading that in the distant Southwest there are ancient match-stick figures on the walls of desert caves and that some of them are playing the flute. In New Hampshire, where I am now, there's only this dark house, the ghostly statue, the silence of the woods, and the cold winter night falling down in a big hurry.

Food and Happiness

Sadness and good food are incompatible. The old sages knew that wine lets the tongue loose, but one can grow melancholy with even the best bottle, especially as one grows older. The appearance of food, however, brings instant happiness. A *paella,* a *choucroute garnie,* a pot of *tripes à la mode de Caen,* and so many other dishes of peasant origin guarantee merriment. The best talk is around that table. Poetry and wisdom are its company. The true Muses are cooks. Cats and dogs don't stay far from the busy kitchen. Heaven is a pot of chili simmering on the stove. If I were to write about the happiest days of my life, many of them would have to do with food and wine and a table full of friends.

> *Homer never wrote on an empty stomach.*
>
> —Rabelais

One could compose an autobiography mentioning every memorable meal in one's life and it would probably make better reading than what one ordinarily gets. Honestly, what would you rather have, the description of a first kiss or of stuffed cabbage done to perfection?

I have to admit, I remember better what I've eaten than what I've thought. My memory is especially vivid about those far-off days from 1944 to 1949 in Yugoslavia, when we were mostly starving. The black market flourished. Women exchanged their wedding rings and silk underwear for hams.

Written for the special issue of *Antaeus* on food, wine, and the art of eating and published in 1992.

Occasionally someone invited us to an illicit feast on a day everyone else was hungry.

I'll begin with the day I realized that there was more to food than just stuffing yourself. I was nine years old. I ate Dobrosav Cvetković's *burek*, and I can still see it and taste it when I close my eyes.

A *burek* is a kind of pie made with phyllo dough and stuffed with either ground meat, cheese, or spinach. It is eaten everywhere in the Near East and the Balkans. Like pizza today, it's usually good no matter where you get it, but it can also be a work of art. My father said that when Dobrosav retired from his bakery in Skopje, the mayor and his cronies, after realizing that he was gone, sent a police warrant after him. The cops brought him back in handcuffs! "Dobrosav," they said visiting him in jail, "how can you do a thing like that to us? At least make us one last *burek*, and then you can go wherever your heart desires."

I ate that famous *burek* forty-four years ago on a cold winter morning with snow falling. Dobrosav made it illegally in his kitchen and sold it to select customers, who used to knock on his door and enter looking like foreign agents making a pickup. The day I was his guest—for the sake of my poor exiled father who was so good to Dobrosav—the *burek* came with meat. I ate every greasy crumb that fell out of my mouth on the table while old Dobrosav studied me the way a cat studies a bird in a cage. He wanted my opinion. I understood this was no fluke. Dobrosav knew something other *burek* makers did not. I believe I told him so. This was my first passionate outburst to a cook.

Then there was my aunt, Ivanka Bajalović. Every time I wiped my plate clean she shook her head sadly. "One day," she'd say to me, "I'll make so much food you won't be able to finish it." With my appetite in those days that seemed impossible, but she did it! She found a huge pot ordinarily used to make soap and filled it with enough beans to "feed an army," as the neighbors said.

All Serbians, of whatever gender or age, have their own opinion as to how this dish ought to be made. Some folks like it thick, others soupy. Between the two extremes there are many nuances. Almost everybody adds bacon, pork ribs, sausage, paprika, and hot peppers. It's a class thing. The upper classes make it lean, the lower fatty. My aunt, who was educated in London and speaks English with a British accent to this day, made it like a ditchdigger's wife. The beans were spicy hot.

My uncle was one of those wonders of nature everybody envies, a skinny guy who could eat all day long and never gain any weight. I'm sad to admit that I've no idea how much we actually ate that day. Anywhere between three and five platefuls is a good guess. These were European soup plates, nice and roomy, that could take loads of beans. It was a summer afternoon. We were eating on a big terrace watched by nosy neighbors, who kept score. At some point, I remember, I just slid off my chair onto the floor.

I'm dying, it occurred to me. My uncle was still wielding his spoon with his face deep in his plate. There was a kind of hush. In the beginning, everybody talked and kidded around, but now my aunt was exhausted and had gone in to lie down. There were still plenty of beans, but I was through. I couldn't move. Finally, even my uncle staggered off to bed, and I was left alone, sitting under the table, the heat intolerable, the sun setting, my mind blurry, thinking, This is how a pig must feel.

On May 9, 1950, I asked all my relatives to give me money instead of presents for my birthday. When they did, I spent the entire day going with a friend from one pastry shop to another. We ate huge quantities of cream puffs, custard rolls, *dobos torta,* rum balls, pishingers, strudel with poppy seed, and other Viennese and Hungarian pastries. At dusk we had no money left. We were dragging ourselves in the general vicinity of the Belgrade railroad station when a man, out of breath and carrying a large suitcase, overtook us. He wondered if we could carry it to the station for him and we said we could. The suitcase was very heavy and it made a noise as if it was full of silverware or burglar's tools, but we managed somehow to get it to his train. There, he surprised us by paying us handsomely for our good deed. Without a moment's thought we returned to our favorite pastry shop, which was closing at that hour and where the help eyed us with alarm as we ordered more ice cream and cake.

In 1951 I lived an entire summer in a village on the Adriatic coast. Actually, the house my mother, brother, and I roomed at was a considerable distance from the village on a stretch of sandy beach. Our landlady, a war widow, was a fabulous cook. In her home I ate squid for the first time and began my lifelong love affair with olives. All her fish was grilled with a little olive oil, garlic, and parsley. I still prefer it that way.

My favorite dish was a plate of tiny surf fish called *girice*, which were fried in corn flour. We'd eat them with our fingers, head and all. Since it's no good to swim after lunch, all the guests would take a long siesta. I remember our deliciously cool room, the clean sheets, the soothing sound of the sea, the aftertaste and smell of the fish, and the long naps full of erotic dreams.

There were two females who obsessed me in that place. One was a theater actress from Zagreb in the room next to ours who used to sunbathe with her bikini top removed when our beach was deserted. I would hide in the bushes. The other was our landlady's sixteen-year-old daughter. I sort of tagged along after her. She must have been bored out of her wits to allow a thirteen-year-old boy to keep her company. We used to swim out to a rock in the bay where there were wild grapes. We'd lie sunbathing and popping the little blue grapes in our mouths. And in the evening, once or twice, there was even a kiss, and then an exquisite risotto with mussels.

> *He that with his soup will drink,*
> *When he's dead won't sleep a wink.*

—Old French Song

In Paris I went to what can only be described as a school for losers. These were youngsters who were not destined for the further glories of French education but were en route to being petty bureaucrats and tradespeople. We ate lunch in school, and the food was mostly tolerable. We even drank red wine. The vegetable soup served on Tuesdays, however, was out of this world. One of the fat ladies I saw milling in the kitchen must have been a southerner, because the soup had a touch of Provence. For some reason, the other kids didn't care for it. Since the school rule was that you had to *manger* everything on your plate, and since I loved the soup so much, my neighbors at the table would let me have theirs. I'd end up eating three or four servings of that thick concoction with tomatoes, green and yellow beans, potatoes, carrots, white beans, noodles, and herbs. After that kind of eating, I usually fell asleep in class after lunch only to be rudely awakened by one of my teachers and ordered to a blackboard already covered with numbers. I'd stand there bewildered and feeling sleepy while time changed into eternity and nobody budged or said anything. My only solace was the lingering taste in my mouth of that divine soup.

Some years back I found myself in Genoa at an elegant reception in Palazzo Doria talking with the Communist mayor. "I love American food," he blurted out to me after I mentioned enjoying the local cuisine. I asked him what he had in mind. "I love potato chips," he told me. I had to agree, potato chips were pretty good.

When we came to the United States in 1954, it now seems as if that's all my brother and I ate. We sat in front of the TV eating potato chips out of huge bags. Our parents approved. We were learning English and being American. It's a wonder we have any teeth left today. We visited the neighborhood supermarket twice a day to sightsee the junk food. There were so many things to taste, and we were interested in all of them. There was deviled ham, marshmallows, Spam, Hawaiian Punch, Fig Newtons, V-8 Juice, Mounds Bars, Planter's Peanuts, and so much else, all good. Everything was good in America except for Wonder Bread, which we found disgusting.

It took me a few years to come to my senses. One day I met Salvatore. He told me I ate like a dumb shit and took me home to his mother. Sal and his three brothers were all well employed, unmarried, living at home, and giving their paychecks to Mom. The father was dead, so there were just these four boys to feed. She did not stop cooking. Every meal was like a peasant wedding feast. Of course, her sons didn't appreciate it as far as she was concerned. "Are you crazy, Mom?" they'd shout in a chorus each time she brought in another steaming dish. The old lady didn't flinch. The day I came she was happy to have someone else at the table who was more appreciative, and I did not spare the compliments.

She cooked southern Italian dishes. Lots of olive oil and garlic. I recollect with a sense of heightened consciousness her linguine with anchovies. We drank red Sicilian wine with it. She'd put several open bottles on the table before the start of the meal. I never saw anything like it. She'd lie to us and say there was nothing more to eat, so we'd have at least two helpings, and then she'd bring out some sausage and peppers, and after that some kind of roast.

After the meal we'd remain at the table, drinking and listening to old records of Beniamino Gigli and Feruccio Tagliavini. The old lady would still be around, urging on us a little more cheese, a little more cake. And then, just when we thought she had given up and gone to bed, she'd surprise us by bringing out a dish of fresh figs.

My late father, who never in his life refused another helping at the table, had a peculiarity common among gastronomes. The more he ate the more he talked about food. My mother was always amazed. We'd be done with a huge turkey roasted over sauerkraut and my father would begin reminiscing about a little breakfastlike sausage he'd had in some village on the Romanian border in 1929, or a fish soup a blind woman made for him in Marseilles in 1945. Well, she wasn't completely blind, and besides she was pretty to look at—in any case, after three or four stories like that we'd be hungry again. My father had a theory that if you were still hungry, say for a hot dog, after a meal at Lutèce, that meant that you were extraordinarily healthy. If a casual visitor to your house was not eating and drinking three minutes after his arrival, you had no manners. Of people who had no interest in food, he had absolutely no comprehension. He'd ask them questions like an anthropologist, and go away seriously puzzled and worried.

He told me toward the end of his life that the greatest mistake he ever made was accepting his doctor's advice to eat and drink less after he passed seventy-five. He felt terrible until he went back to his old ways.

One day we are walking up Second Avenue and talking. We get into an elaborate philosophical argument, as we often do. I feel as if I've understood everything! I'm inspired! I'm quoting Kant, Descartes, Wittgenstein, when I notice he's no longer with me. I look around and locate him a block back staring into a shop window. I'm kind of pissed, especially since I have to walk back to where he's standing, since he doesn't move or answer my shouts. Finally, I tap him on the shoulder and he looks at me, dazed. "Can you believe that?," he says and points to a window full of Hungarian smoked sausages, salamis, and pork rinds.

My friend, Mike DePorte, whose grandfather was a famous St. Petersburg lawyer and who in his arguments combines a Dostoevskian probity with his grandfather's jurisprudence, claims that such an obsession with food is the best proof we have of the existence of the soul. Ergo, long after the body is satisfied, the soul is not. "Does that mean," I asked him, "that the soul is never satisfied?" He has not given me his answer yet. My own notion is that it is a supreme sign of happiness. When our souls are happy, they talk about food.

The Little Venus of the Eskimos

You just go on your nerve

—Frank O'Hara

In India, I remember reading as a child, there once lived people who were called Sciapodes. They had a single large foot on which they moved with great speed and which they also employed as an umbrella against the burning sun. The rest of their marvelous lives was up to the reader to imagine. The book was full of such creatures. I kept turning its pages, reading the brief descriptions and carefully examining the drawings. There was Cerberus, the dog with three heads, the Centaur, the Chinese Dragon, the Manticora, which has the face of a man, the body of a lion, and a tail like the sting of a scorpion, and many other wonders. They resembled, I realized years later, the creations of Cadavre Exquis, the surrealist game of chance. I was also reminded of Max Ernst's surrealist novels in collage where bird wings sprout from people's backs and rooster-headed men carry off naked women.

The history of these fabulous beings is dateless. They are found in the oldest mythologies and in all cultures. Their origins vary. Some are very probably symbolic representations of theological ideas by long forgotten sects and alchemist schools for whom the marriage of opposite elements was the guiding idea. Others, I'd like to believe, are the products of sheer fantasy, the liar's art, and our fascination with the grotesque image of the body. In both cases, they are the earliest instances of the collage aesthetic. Mythological zoos testify to our curiosity about the outcome of the sexual embrace of

Written in 1993 for an exhibition at the Drawing Center in New York City called "The Return of Cadavre Exquis."

different species. They are the earliest examples of the collaboration of dream and intellect for the sake of putting appearances into doubt.

Were these visual oxymorons of ancient bestiaries first imagined and then drawn, or was it the other way around? Did one start drawing a head and the hand took off on its own, as it does in automatic writing? It's possible, although I don't have a lot of faith in automatic writing, with its aping of mediums and their trances. All my attempts at opening the floodgates of my psyche were unimpressive. "You need a certain state of vacancy for the marvelous to condescend to visit you," said Benjamin Peret. Very well and thanks for the advice, but I have my doubts. The reputation of the unconscious as the endless source of poetry is over-rated. The first rule for a poet must be, cheat on your unconscious and your dreams.

It was Octavio Paz, I believe, who told me the story about going to visit André Breton in Paris after the War. He was admitted and told to wait because the poet was engaged. Indeed, from the living room where he was seated, he could see Breton writing furiously in his study. After a while he came out, and they greeted each other and set out to have lunch in a nearby restaurant.

"What were you working on, maître?" Paz inquired as they were strolling to their destination.

"I was doing some automatic writing," Breton replied.

"But," Paz exclaimed in astonishment, "I saw you erase repeatedly!"

"It wasn't automatic enough," Breton assured the young poet.

I must admit to being shocked, too, when I heard the story. I thought I was the only one who did that. There have always been two opposite and contradictory approaches to chance operations. In the first, one devises systems to take words at random out of a dictionary or writes poems with scissors, old newspapers, and paste. The words found in either manner are not tampered with. The poem is truly the product of blind chance. All mechanical chance operations, from Dada's picking words out of a hat to the compositions of John Cage and the poems of Jackson Mac Low, work something like that. There is no cheating. These people are as honest and as scrupulous as the practitioners of photo realism. I mean, they are both suspicious of the imagination. They handle chance with a Buddhist's disinterestedness of mind and do not allow it to be contaminated by the impurities of desire.

My entire practice, on the other hand, consists of submitting to chance only to cheat on it. I agree with Vincent Huidobro who said long ago: "Chance is fine when you're dealt five aces or at least four queens. Otherwise, forget it." I, for example, may pull a book from my bookshelf and, opening it anywhere, take out a word or a phrase. Then, to find another bit of language to go along with my first find, I may grab another book or peek into one of my notebooks and get something like this:

> he rips some papers
> forest
> whispers
> telephone book
> a child's heart
> the mouse has a nest
> concert piano
> lost innocence
> my mother's mourning dress

Once the words are on the page, however, I let them play off each other. In the house of correction called sense, where language and art serve their sentences, the words are making whoopee.

Innocence

Someone rips a telephone book in half.
The mouse has a nest in a concert piano.

In a forest of whispers,
A child's heart,
The mother's mourning dress.

This is more interesting. I'm beginning to feel that there are real possibilities here. To see what comes next, I'll call on chance for help again. My premise in this activity is that the poet finds poetry in what comes by accident. It's a complete revision of what we usually mean by creativity.

Twenty years ago, James Tate and I collaborated on some poems in the following manner: We'd take a word or a phrase and then we'd turn ourselves into a "pinball machine of associations," as Paul Auster would say. For example, the word "match" and the word "jail" would become "matchstick jail." At some point we'd stop and see what we had. We'd even do a bit of literary analysis. We'd revise, free associate again, and watch an unknown poem begin to take shape. At some moments we felt as if we were one person; at others, one of us was the inspired poet and the other the cold-blooded critic.

Russell Edson, who with James Tate and John Ashbery is one of our greatest believers in lucky finds, says, "This kind of creation needs to be done as rapidly as possible. Any hesitation causes it to lose its believability, its special reality." I have the same experience. One doesn't come up with phrases like Tate's "the wheelchair butterfly" or Bill Knott's "razorblade choir" by way of a leisurely Cartesian meditation. They are as much a surprise to the poet as they will be to the future reader.

I open myself to chance in order to invite the unknown. I'm not sure whether it's fate or chance that dogs me, but something does. I'm like a reader of tea leaves in that store on the corner. In Madame Esmeralda's metaphysics, there is a recognition scene, too. Clairvoyants believe that there are lucky days, moments when one's divinatory abilities are especially acute. Today, one says to oneself, I'm the waking dream, the source of the magical river! I see the hand that guides fate. The miraculous thing is that the tea leaves and the poem always end up by resembling me. Here is a near-portrait, the story of my life, and I've no idea how they got there.

If you worship in the Church of Art with a Message, stay away. Chance operations make trouble, promote ambiguity, spit on dogmatism of any kind. Everything from our ideas of identity to our ideas of cause and effect are cheerfully undermined. Surrealist games are the greatest blasphemy yet conceived by the arts against the arts. In them, the disordering of the senses is given ontological status. Chance brings a funhouse mirror to reality. They used to burn people at the stake for far less.

There has never been a poet who didn't believe in a stroke of luck. What is an occasional poem but a quick convergence of unforeseen bits of language? That's what Catullus and Frank O'Hara are all about. Only literary critics do not know that poems mostly write themselves. Metaphors and similes owe everything to chance. A poet cannot will a memorable comparison. These things just pop into somebody's head. In the past one thanked the gods or the Muse for it, but all along chance has been passing out freebies. Pierce claimed that only by granting the occurrence of chance events can one account for the diversity of the universe. The same is true of art and literature.

How does one recognize that blind accident has given one poetry? This is what puzzles me. What is it that guides the eye or the ear to accept what appears at first ugly or nonsensical? One says to oneself many times while writing, what I have here I do not understand at all, but I'm going to keep it no matter what.

> Painter of doll faces
> Here's a window where my soul
> Used to peek out at night
> At the quickly improvised gallows

If there's no such a thing as an aesthetic sense, how does one pick and choose among the various products of chance and decide some are worthless and some are not? Obviously, the history of modern art and literature has accustomed the eye and ear to the unexpected. We are happy, or so we believe, to reorient our vision, to accept any outrage. Is it still our old fascination with freak shows that drives us, or are formal aesthetic considerations just as important?

No doubt both. Successful chance operations stress the ambiguous origin and complex nature of any work of art or literature. The art object is always a collaboration of will and chance, but like our sense of humor, it eludes analysis. There has never been an adequate definition of why something is funny or why something is beautiful, and yet we often laugh and make poems and paintings that reassemble reality in new and unpredictably pleasing ways.

What shocks us more in the end, what we see or what we hear? Is the ear more avant-garde or the eye? Surrealist art has found more admirers than surrealist poetry, so it must be the eye. It's the new image that both painters and poets have dreamed of in this century, an image that would be ahead of our ideas and our desires, an image magnificent in its shock and its irreverence. Perhaps some new Temptation of Saint Anthony, in which the holy martyr praying in the desert would be surrounded by the rioting menagerie of exquisite corpses instead of traditional demons?

Surrealists intuited that the creation of the world is not yet finished. The Chaos spoken of in ancient creation myths has not said its last word. Chance continues to be one of the manifestations of cosmic mystery. The other one is mathematics. We are crucified in awe between freedom and necessity. The future is the forever unfolding game of Cadavre Exquis.

In the meantime, like the song says, "I've got my mojo working."

Fried Sausage

It is a fact, you singers of the lilies of the field, that the smell of fried sausage means nothing to you.

—Unknown author

The word *nature* has always had for me, a city boy, unpleasant didactic connotations. It was the place where our mothers and our schools took us occasionally so we could get some fresh air. We'd be led to a spot with lots of trees and a pretty view, where we would be ordered to breathe deeply and cleanse our lungs of the foul city air. "Isn't nature beautiful?" my mother or my schoolteacher would exclaim. And we pretended to agree, thinking meanwhile, Times Square on a Saturday night is the place to be. A city with its crowds, traffic, movies, saloons, jazz clubs, beggars, muggers, and yes, the smell of fried sausage, has always been more attractive to me. Nature is where yokels lived, *idiotikos*, as ancient Greeks used to call the unfortunates who lived outside the polis. I don't mind the middle of the ocean, or a garden choked with hot peppers, eggplants, and tomatoes, but idealized nature has always struck me as a fool's paradise.

> The cow lets fall an even
> Golden stream of shit,
> Terence, you lie under
> And never mind a bit of it.

I forget where I read this gem, but these verses always come to my mind when I read pastoral poetry. Very nice, one

---

Written in 1992 for the special issue of the *Ohio Review* on art and nature.

says to oneself, but what about the farmer beyond that gorgeous meadow who works seven days a week from morning to night and is still starving? What about his sickly wife and their boy, who tortures cats? As my father used to say, if country living was any good, all these cities would not be so packed. Now, of course, I live in the boonies. I have been in New Hampshire almost twenty years and in my walks through the woods I regularly bump into Emerson and Thoreau. We nod to each other in a friendly way and go our separate ways. It's true I've often made fun of them behind their backs. I've imagined Waldo as the cow certain poets milk. I've guffawed at some of Henry's rhapsodizing. I could never free myself from the thought that Nature is that which is slowly killing me. In addition, any philosophy of Nature that doesn't include nude picnics and rolling in the hay leaves me cold. Still and all, living here as I do, where their feet and eyes have roamed, who else do I have to argue with but these two illustrious and fine old neighbors?

This is how I see it. There are three ways of thinking about the world. You can think about the Cosmos (as the Greeks did), you can think about History (as the Hebrews did), and since the late eighteenth century you can think about Nature. The choice is yours. Where do you prefer to find (or not find) the meaning of your life? And do you include God on the menu? I myself fancy the cosmic angle. The brain-chilling infinities and silences of modern astronomy and Pascalian thought impress me deeply, except that I'm also a child of History. I've seen tanks, piles of corpses, and people strung from lampposts with my own eyes. As for Nature so-called, it's a product of Romantic utopias: noble savage, Rousseau, earthly paradise in the manner of Gauguin, the projects of Charles Fourier, our Transcendentalists, and so forth. No longer the golden city but a lush meadow where happy humans and sheep gambol.

Most American writers on Nature partake of that utopian strain and its Manichaeanism. It's always the machine versus the garden, freedom versus confinement, God in Nature and the devil in the city. The city with its contradictions, its history, its freedom and exhilaration is godless and un-American.

Only a few of our poets have praised it. Frank O'Hara comes to mind, but while he sipped beer at Cedar Tavern, it seems that all his contemporaries went fishing.

Can we have modern literature without a city? Can we write about history without quarreling with nature? Plenty of poets think we can, but I doubt it.

Until we resolve these questions, a nap in a hammock on a summer afternoon is highly recommended. "The universe is breaking up, losing all hope of a single design," I read somewhere recently. History has not ended, despite recent predictions to the contrary, but is proceeding, as it always has, on its bloody way. Our options are limited. We can either sign hymns or grind our teeth, as Zbigniew Herbert pointed out. I do both.

"A sausage of angel and beast," Nicanor Parra called human beings. Is that why the sows are sighing in the afternoon heat in their pens across the road? They know the score. Pigs, I'm convinced, despite what Plato said about dogs, are the most philosophical of all animals. Such a fine brain, such an alert beginning, but then all that gluttony leading to the abyss of laziness. If a sow can still in rare moments ponder, what tragic, Shakespearean peaks it must reach. I, too, as a late twentieth-century sufferer of all the unforeseen consequences of all the utopian projects of the last two hundred years, have a horror of generalizations, especially when they come wrapped in good intentions. Nature as experience—making a tomato salad, say, with young mozzarella, fresh basil leaves, and olive oil—is better than any idea about Nature.

"It is a bone on which reason breaks its teeth," Machado said of the otherness of everything we see. Not only reason, I want to shout, but our hearts too. When it comes to Being and Nature and even History, all of us are toothless. In the meantime, here's a Polish song to sing in a hammock while falling asleep and dreaming of that tomato salad:

> Down the road the children go,
> a sister and a brother,
> and they cannot help but wonder
> at the beauty of the world.

Bicycle Thieves

Bad luck is the only luck I ever had

—Old blues song

From its title, which forewarns us that a bike will be stolen, everything is inevitable in this film. "To hell with poverty," says the man who has gotten a job after two years of waiting. His bike will be stolen and finding it will be like looking for a needle in a haystack. "We find it or we don't eat," says the man to his son, and there's your plot, with a weight of inevitability worthy of a Greek tragedy.

This fellow in a shabby suit and the streets and buildings in downtown Rome, all that looked familiar. There are parts of all large European cities that are almost identical in architecture. My childhood took place among such late nineteenth-century apartment houses and office buildings in Belgrade, Yugoslavia. After the war they were gray and rundown, their walls peeling.

I first saw *The Bicycle Thief* there in the late 1940s. Ordinarily I cared only for American films, Westerns especially, but they were rarely imported in the glory days of Stalinism. We mostly saw Soviet films and a few so-called progressive French and Italian ones. The sad thing about socialist realism in the arts is that even a child of ten finds its idealized characters and wholesome message hopelessly boring. I remember going to De Sica's film with considerable suspicion and being surprised to be so deeply moved.

Like the people in the film, most of the families I knew were poor and unemployed, and had little to eat. Both the young and the old stole. I once went into a bakery, took a chunk of bread from the counter, and ran out with customers in pursuit. There are grandmothers in that neighborhood who still accuse me, more than forty years later, of swiping, on different occasions, a garden hose, an ax, and a baby carriage, and are astonished and annoyed that I still deny it. A movie about stealing bicycles was something I understood perfectly even at that age.

I recollect little of that first viewing of the film except for a few scenes that have remained vivid: The father and the boy after a day of looking for the stolen bicycle decide to splurge and have a meal in a trattoria. There is a rich kid at the next table, eating carefully with a fork and knife in the company of his family, who keeps turning and watching Bruno gobble his food. He wears the kind of clothes boys of that social class used to wear even in postwar Communist Belgrade. We'd see one of them in a sailor suit holding the hand of his mother on the street. They were always with their mothers; otherwise they would have been beaten up. In the meantime, there would be a lot of rubbernecking back and forth, just as in the movie.

I also remember the bedsheets the Riccis pawn to get the bicycle out of hock. There are shelves and shelves full of old bedsheets. A man climbs the shelves like a monkey to add the new bundle. Thousands of bedsheets in which people slept and made love. More bedsheets than anyone ever saw. That scene took my breath away every time I saw the movie.

I caught the film several more times over the years, and every time I had the same thought: this is the grainy black and white look of my childhood. The streetcar early Sunday morning, for instance, when they accompany the trash collectors on their rounds. Or the thieves' market in the rain. Or the horse's head bowing down as they stand at the open door of the trattoria. The musicians inside remind me of the Italian prisoners of war who came to our door begging for food. The whole movie is seen through the eyes of a child. Neo-Realism is the way a poor city kid sees the world.

You don't need Hamlets and Lears or assassinated presidents to experience the tragic. This Antonio with his peasant's face dried by the sun has about him a refinement, a gentleness and a deep sense of cosmic injustice worthy of a king in a Greek tragedy. And so does his family! His son is a smart, sensitive boy. He is his father's conscience, we are told, and he is ours, too. And so is the mother with her sad eyes. She too understands everything. De Sica does not sentimentalize these people. They are not angels. His art is in the clear vision of what they are and in the many luminous details.

What makes memory and art durable are the details—or, I should say, the poetry of details. Antonio and Maria riding the bike at dusk from the pawn shop as if they were young lovers. The little kid playing the accordion and his buddy begging while Antonio is putting up the poster of Rita Hayworth. The pervert who wants to buy Bruno a bell at the bike market. The jabbering German seminarians hiding from the rain with Antonio and Bruno. The soup kitchen where the rich purify the souls of the poor from sin before they serve them potatoes and noodles. The father making the son figure out with a stub of a pencil on a small piece of paper how much he would have made on the job he is about to lose.

Each scene not only is visually interesting, but it has a kind of wisdom about it. Like the pots on the stove in the thief's kitchen over which his mother fusses, these people are even poorer than the victims, one quickly realizes! And yet none of it appears staged, nor does it carry a "message." One shudders to think how we Americans would have made the movie! De Sica knows the poor are a thieving lot, but he also knows that there are important differences between thieves. "That boy wouldn't hurt a fly," someone says about the thief, and the audience is laughing.

When Antonio decides to steal a bicycle we understand his reasoning. I need a bicycle to feed my family and here are so many bicycles outside the soccer stadium where a game is just ending. There's a great shot of the father and son sitting on the sidewalk, the crowd of happy faces after their team's victory passing by. We know Antonio will fail, and he does. There are just too many people around. With the first cry of "thief," he will be brought down from the stolen bike. "Nice thing you're teaching your son," says someone in the crowd. But, what precisely, given their experience, would he teach his son? De Sica avoids any neat summations. At the end of the movie the father and son are walking with tears in their eyes holding each other by the hand. They have their love for each other but not much else. But what a love that is!

I'm sure that a lot of Marias in the audience saw the tragedy as the consequence of the wife's not paying the seer for predicting that her husband will get a job. Antonio suspects it, too, and that's why he returns to consult the woman about the stolen bike in the crowded bedroom where everybody listens to everybody else's troubles. He pays her, but now it's too late. The seer says and repeats, "Either you find it now or you never will," and we understand that it's not only the bike she means as she glances at the window beyond which there is Rome and the whole world.

Lady Be Good

Sweet and lovely lady be good . . . I'm lost in this great big city.
Won't you please have a little pity?

—Ira & George Gershwin

"That thing came from a maximum security penitentiary," she told me.

I could not say what kind of metal it was made of or what it had originally been used for. Part of a rusty machine, some kind of pin, I touched it with my tongue and was surprised by how cold it felt. Like the stone floor in a solitary, I thought.

"One writes the years of one's imprisonment with such an object," I said.

"One must keep it hidden at all times," she replied with an air of mystery.

The man who left it with her was her lover for a month. That had been some years earlier.

"He used to scratch my back at night with it," she told me.

She wore a flowered silk robe and red slippers on her bare feet. They kept falling off when she crossed her legs. I still held the metal object in my hand. I kept wondering if she would give it to me, if I asked for it, if I pretended to beg.

Her robe was slightly open. I put the object on the table between us. Outside it was beginning to rain. She jumped to close the windows, giving me a peek, in the process, of her breasts and her long legs. Soon it was raining so hard, the room grew dark.

She talked and I listened.

"I have the impression," she said to me, "that in my life

This selection is an excerpt from a memoir in progress. This essay was published in *Boulevard* in 1993.

there have been more nights than days. It was like night came, and then, just as the new day was about to break, another night would follow immediately in its wake.

"I forget the face of my lovers because it has always been night. Only their bodies still keep their ghostly whiteness for me. I want to touch them, but I no longer have the right."

Just before I left she turned on a single table lamp to read me a poem, the plot of which I still remember.

In the woods, one Sunday when they were children, she and her brother came upon a couple lying on the ground. Hand in hand, afraid themselves of being lost, they saw, what they first surmised was a patch of snow. In a spot rarely visited, with the wind sighing over the new leaves, they came upon the embraced ones, the two naked people clutching each other on the cold ground. It was spring. The woods had already a bit of purple shade. There was a bird, too, singing and falling silent as they stole by.

It was still raining when I came out on the street. I was still twenty years old and she was at least forty. Our connection was poetry; which we both wrote and showed to each other. I stopped by her place in late afternoons, often unannounced. It was all very simple. I was attracted to her, I also liked her stories, so I came. Otherwise, I knew nothing about her, except that she grew up in some place like Minnesota or Montana and that she had lived in Europe for a long time. She had the tired eyes and faded beauty of someone whose life had many ups and downs. She could've been a rich expatriate living alone and drinking heavily in some villa in Florence. She could've been a nightclub singer of another era. In any case, she was always alone, letting me visit for hours, and then without a warning, throwing me out, supposedly just remembering that someone was coming to see her or that she had an appointment to keep.

A couple of times I spied on her from across the street. The first time she went out in a great hurry, wearing a wide-brimmed hat and dark glasses, and caught a cab on the corner. The next time she didn't come out at all. A small boy with glasses entered her brownstone, and then a young couple carrying grocery bags. At ten her lights were still on, so I crossed the street and found the front door unlocked. I went up without a thought in my head, only a powerful desire to see her. On the third floor, I put my ear to her door. There was not a sound to be heard. I wanted to knock, I should have knocked, but instead I stood there, listening to my heart beat wildly. After a long wait, I went home.

Next door to where I lived on East 13th Street, there was a rundown brownstone with a basement from which a street-vendor supplier operated. Derelicts, if they were hired, sold umbrellas, ties, fake Swiss watches, miracle potato peelers, and other such junk, up and down 14th Street. The boss looked like Anthony Quinn's Zampano, the circus artist who breaks heavy chains in *La Strada*. He examined his men in the morning and chased away the ones who appeared too shabby, too sickly, or who were simply too drunk. Every time he noticed me watching, he gave me a nasty look that said, "I'm going to wring your neck kid, one of these days!"

In the evening, and even late into the night, he'd be there outside his establishment, eyeing me evilly as I went by. I attributed my strange dreams to his presence.

I dreamt, for instance, that I was in a dressing room of some kind. It could've been vaudeville, a strip joint, a circus, or perhaps a sports arena. The mirrors had cracks in them and the sofa had its stuffing showing. I suspected there were wrestlers, dancers, acrobats, transvestites about to return. When she walked in, I was very surprised. She wore a low-cut black dress with thin straps and did not appear to see me. She lay down on the sofa with her eyes closed as if extremely, hopelessly tired. As I drew close, the powerful reality of her body in my dream surprised me even more. I who had never seen her naked felt in that instant before waking that I knew her arms, legs, and mouth as if I had covered them with kisses many times.

After one such dream I wrote a poem that I still vaguely recollect. In a field next to the town dump a man and a woman sit drinking until the heat makes them take their clothes off. There's an old tub thrown in the tall weeds where she goes to sit and pretends to wash herself. The man dances around her playing the wine bottle as if it were a goatherd's flute. When some birds fly over them, she throws her head back, so that her breasts bounce in full view above the rusty rim of the tub. He, meanwhile, is sitting on the ground, looking for a thorn in his feet, his cock stiff between his hairy legs.

I called the poem "Pastoral" and thought of showing it to her but never summoned the courage to, telling myself that it was not very good, that it was incomprehensible and kind of embarrassing.

She had a cousin who counted leaves all day long, she told me. He was mad and they had plenty of trees. After a while, he'd grow tired and would sit down on the ground, his finger still pointing up, his lips still moving. It was hard to tell one leaf from another with the night coming, he confided to her once. She imagined a figure with many zeros lengthening in his head like a comet's tail. While she was telling me this she kept looking at me with a little smile as if I were her mad cousin.

On another occasion she told me how her mother liked walking barefoot in the rain. Everyone on the street would run for cover and stand in doorways watching her take off her shoes and stockings in plain view with the rain pouring down. They'd stroll together barefoot, kicking the puddles with all those disapproving faces watching.

Where was that? I wanted to know, but just then, and for the first time, she asked me to stay for dinner. She would make squid and rice and I would help her. I told her that I was crazy about squid and rice. And it was true. When it came to food, music, books, I was pretty sophisticated. In everything else I was a lost sheep in the woods.

Since I'm writing this thirty years later, I'm more aware and less embarrassed about my shyness then. I remember watching her clean the squid, expertly removing the delicate, fin-like bones. I stood right behind her. Her hands were surprisingly ugly. The fingernails appeared bitten, and viciously at that. Strong, brutal hands so much in contrast with the back of her neck which was white and soft. I thought of girls who sat in front of me in grade school bending over their exams. I was so close, my lips lightly brushing her pale blonde hair, I'm astonished I didn't kiss her.

I can still relive that moment with undiminished clarity. I can still peek down her robe and see her full breasts down to their nipples. She was now chopping onions, tears were running down her face. She was laughing and explaining to me the Spanish peasant recipe she was using as I hovered over her.

Is that why she always had that little smile for me? She knew, of course, what was going on in my head and in my pants, and that was the fun of it for her.

Later, over wine and cheese, I showed her a poem I had just written. It was not the one about the naked lady in a tub. It went like this:

> The Holy Virgin lives over the grocery store.
> She wears a Salvation Army uniform even when she
>   steps out to throw the garbage out.
> Mice scurry around her feet.
> St. John the Baptist has a pigeon coop on the roof.
> His martyrdom includes emptying bedpans in a hospital.
> One night he knocks on her door and walks right in.
> There's a dressmaker's dummy to greet him,
> Ugly little pins stuck in it.
> She is lying in bed with eyes closed.
> The room is dark, the sky is windy and cloudy.
> Her eyes are still tightly closed.

Before she had time to comment on my awkward blasphemy, the phone rang in the next room, she answered it, and told me, I must leave immediately because she had to go out.

That night I woke with a huge hard-on. I wanted to go over to her place. I was absolutely certain in that moment that she was expecting me to do just that. Her door would open even before I would touch it. It'd be pitch dark. She'd lead me by the hand and I wouldn't make a sound, even with her naked body brushing against me and her hand gripping mine so hard. We'd be like two blind people, two blind lovers in an unfamiliar world.

I dressed quickly and without tying my shoes ran into the street. It was long past midnight. The streets were empty and the summer night was warm and humid. Her windows were dark, her front door locked. I sat on the steps, tied my shoelaces, and had a smoke. Since I was not in the mood for bed, I took a walk. Dark streets, dark trees, but then up ahead in the next block, there was noise and lights. A party was in progress, the crowd had even spilled onto the sidewalk. The guests were dressed as if they had gone to a wedding, or the opera. They were in high spirits.

I did not hesitate, I walked right in. The entrance was packed like a rush-hour subway, I had to squeeze from room to room, from floor to floor. Everybody was busy talking and nobody was paying attention to me. I wanted to get a drink, but I couldn't find the bar. I opened a wrong door and found a white-haired man in a tuxedo puking in the toliet. I opened another and found a black labrador tied to the radiator in a room no bigger than a closet. He was happy to see me. I would not have minded staying with him, but all of a sudden, I had a hunch that she might be there at the party.

Again, I looked everywhere. I even got to the roof where I found a couple tottering and kissing close to the edge. Finally, I asked a drunk woman everybody called Marilyn where the drinks were coming from. She handed over a bottle of Irish whiskey without saying a word. She was with an older man who kept whispering in her ear and giving me unfriendly looks. I took the bottle into the living room and pushed my way into the corner. I stood there drinking and watching the people. I had no idea who they were or what the occasion was, and I didn't care. The women seemed uncommonly beautiful. They were all accompanied. Their escorts made them titter or gaze at them with endless admiration.

They should all be in bed screwing, I thought. I was drinking heavily and expecting her to come into view. "We'll fuck right here on the floor," I told a neighbor. The fellow gave me a wary look. I said it again louder. "I'm going to start taking my clothes off right now so I'm ready when she arrives," I warned him. More people were watching me now. I was already unbuttoning my shirt and loosening up my belt.

"It's him," someone shouted, and they all looked in another direction. Someone had just arrived and they were all waving to him. It seemed he could only stay a short time. I couldn't even see the man, but he was obviously a big deal. Suddenly, I felt very tired. I sat on the floor, took another long swig out of the bottle and closed my eyes. I still had the lovely premonition that she'd come. She'd touch my cheek letting her long red nails scratch me a little. I'd open my eyes and greet that little smile of hers with a little smile of my own.

I counted to a hundred very slowly, then to another hundred, even more slowly.

"You must leave now," said the black maid who woke me. I obeyed instantly. The living room was empty and so were the stairs. On the street there was the hush of early Sunday morning; at home, a mouse dead in the kitchen trap with a tiny trickle of blood out of its mouth.

I waited a week. I went to my job selling dress shirts at Stern's Department Store on 42nd Street. I wore a white shirt and tie myself and was as always expected to be extremely polite with customers. Men were no problem, but the women that week drove me nuts. I'd show them a shirt and they'd notice a nonexistent spot on the collar. I'd show them another, but the spot would be somewhere else. If I talked back, they'd complain to the manager who'd chew me out in front of them even though he knew I was right.

In the evening I made the round of local saloons to find my friend Sal and complain about women.

"Perfect creatures," Sal replied every time. He loved them all and refused to entertain the slightest disparagement of the femal sex.

Somebody at the bar would object, mentioning some sourpuss in the neighborhood. "How about her?"

A real bitch, everybody would agree.

"She just needs the right kind of loving," was Sal's opinion. He thought the *Kama Sutra* should be read to little children.

As for my difficulties with Miss X, he told me over and over again that I was a complete jerk.

The afternoon I was to make my last visit to the house of West 12th Street, I carried a bottle of fine French wine and a can of pâté. I had just gotten some money from my father and was in a jaunty mood. I expected us to sit and drink as always. Billie Holiday or Lester Young would be playing on the phonograph with the sound turned down low. "Blue Lester," or "Lady Be Good," perhaps. The night would slowly come and she would not turn on the lights. I would change records, picking out the saddest songs. We'd listen to "Moanin' Low," and "Mean to Me," and the night would fall. I would come over to where she was sitting and bury my head between her legs. Or, I'd wait till we couldn't see each other and tell her I loved her. I felt reckless and giddy with confidence.

The front door was unlocked, so I ran upstairs two steps at a time and knocked. There was no answer, so I banged on the door with my fist. Finally I heard heavy steps, the door opened; a man who appeared to have been sleeping stood there. He was my age. He even looked like me. His T-shirt, I remember, was wet with sweat. He didn't say anything. He expected me to say something, and I just muttered an apology and quickly walked downstairs.

I never went back though I meant to. I have no idea to this day who the woman was or the man who opened the door. I looked for her name in literary journals over the years, but I never found her. I thought of her recently, walking on West 12th Street. It reminded me that I still have a part of a poem she wrote. It's typed on the stationery of Hotel Drake, Chicago, and has just these eight lines:

> Whoever has faith in love
> And goes wherever her feet take her
> In the evening crowd,
> Hoping to be tapped on the shoulder
> By a stranger, whispering already,
> I must tell you of the many things
> That lie heavy on my heart
> Of which I have kept silent so long . . .

The rest of the poem I lost moving from New York to San Francisco many years ago.

Elegy in a Spider's Web

In a letter to Hannah Arendt, Karl Jaspers describes how the philosopher Spinoza used to amuse himself by placing flies in a spider's web, then adding two spiders so he could watch them fight over the flies. "Very strange and difficult to interpret," concludes Jasper. As it turns out, this was the only time the otherwise somber philosopher was known to laugh.

A friend from Yugoslavia called me about a year ago and said, "Charlie, why don't you come home and hate with your own people?

I knew he was pulling my leg, but I was shocked nevertheless. I told him that I was never very good at hating, that I've managed to loathe a few individuals here and there, but had never managed to progress to hating whole peoples.

"In that case," he replied, "you're missing out on the greatest happiness one can have in life."

I'm surprised that there is no History of Stupidity. I envision a work of many volumes, encyclopedic, cumulative, with an index listing millions of names. I only have to think about history for a moment or two before I realize the absolute necessity of such a book. I do not underestimate the influence of religion, nationalism, economics, personal ambition, and even chance on events, but the historian who does not admit that men are also fools has not really understood his subject.

Watching Yugoslavia dismember itself, for instance, is like

A shorter version of this essay appeared in "The New Republic" in 1993.

watching a man mutilate himself in public. He has already managed to make himself legless, armless, and blind, and now in his frenzy he's struggling to tear his heart out with his teeth. Between bites he shouts to us that he is a martyr for a holy cause, but we know that he is mad, that he is monstrously stupid. People tell me I predicted the tragedy years ago. This required no extraordinary wisdom. If our own specialists in ethnic pride in the United States ever start shouting that they can't live with each other, we can expect the same bloodshed to follow. For that reason, what amazed me in the case of Yugoslavia was the readiness with which our intellectuals accepted as legitimate the claim of every nationalist there. The desirability of breaking up into ethnic and religious states a country that had existed since 1918 and that had complicated internal and outside agreements was welcomed with unreserved enthusiasm by everybody from the *New York Times* to the German government. It probably takes much longer to get a fried chicken franchise then it took to convince the world that Yugoslavia should be replaced by as many little states as the natives desired.

> *Isn't "we" the problem, that little word "we" (which I distrust so profoundly, which I would forbid the individual man to use).*
> —Witold Gombrowicz

Dr. Frankenstein's descendants do not dig up fresh graves anymore on dark and stormy nights to make monsters. They stay home and study national history, making up lists of past wrongs. We hear people say in Yugoslavia, "I didn't used to hate them, but after I read what they've been doing to us, I'd like see them all dead."

Nationalism is a self-constructed cage in which family members can huddle in safety when they're not growling and barking at someone outside the cage. One people baring their teeth at all comers is the dream of every nationalist and religious fanatic the world over. The real horror movie monsters would run at the sight of these people, who only yesterday were someone's quiet and kind neighbors and who will probably resume being that after the killing is done.

What are you? Americans ask me. I explain that I was born in Belgrade, that I left when I was fifteen, that we always thought of ourselves as Yugoslavs, that for the last thirty years I have been translating Serbian, Croatian, Slovenian, and Macedonian poets into English, that whatever differences I found among these people delighted me, that I don't give a shit about any of these nationalist leaders and their programs . . .

"Oh, so you're a Serb!" they exclaim triumphantly.

I remember an old interview with Duke Ellington, the interviewer saying to him with complete confidence, you write your music for your own people, and Ellington pretending not to understand, asking what people would that be? The lovers of Beaujolais?

I have more in common with some Patagonian or Chinese lover of Ellington or Emily Dickinson than I have with many of my own people. The proverbial warning, "Too many cooks spoil the broth," was the way I was concocted. I have always considered myself lucky to be that way.

The strange thing is that I find more and more people who do not believe me, who assure me that life has no meaning outside some kind of tribe.

Five of us were sitting in the Brasserie Cluny in Paris writing a protest letter to Milosević and arguing about the wording when one of us remembered that Tito conducted his illegal business for the Comintern in the same brasserie before the war.

Does this crap ever end? someone wondered aloud.

Over the last forty years I've known Russians, Yugoslavs, Hungarians, Poles, Argentines, Chinese, Iranians and a dozen other nationalities, all refugees from murderous regimes. The only people of honor on the whole planet.

This summer in Paris and Amsterdam I met more "traitors," men and women who refused to identify themselves with various nationalist groups in Yugoslavia. They wanted to remain free, outside tribal pieties, and that was their heresy. They are the other orphans of that civil war.

One Sunday on the metro I heard an accordionist play a Serbian song, struck up a conversation with him, and found out he was a war refugee from Croatia. "One of these days," he whispered to me in parting, "the French will get rid of us too and then where will we go?"

His name, to our mutual astonishment, turned out to be Simic too.

Sacrifice the children—an old story, pre-Homeric—so that the nation will endure, to create a legend.

—Aleksander Wat

The destruction of Vukovar and Sarajevo will not be forgiven the Serbs. Whatever moral credit they had as the result of their history they have squandered in these two acts. The suicidal and abysmal idiocy of nationalism is revealed here better than anywhere else. No human being or group of people has the right to pass a death sentence on a city.

"Defend your own, but respect what others have," my grandfather used to say, and he was a highly decorated officer in the First World War and certainly a Serbian patriot. I imagine he would have agreed with me. There will be no happy future for people who have made the innocent suffer.

Here is something we can all count on. Sooner or later our tribe always comes to ask us to agree to murder.

"In the hour of need you walked away from your own people," a fellow I know said to me when I turned down the invitation.

True. I refused to turn my conscience over to the leader of the pack. I continued stubbornly to believe in more than one truth. Only the individual is real, I kept saying over and over again. I praised the outcast, the pariah, while my people were offering me an opportunity to become a part of a mystic whole. I insisted on remaining aloof, self-absorbed, lovingly nursing my suspicions.

"For whom does your poetry speak when you have no tribe anywhere you can call your own?" my interlocutor wanted to know.

"The true poet is never a member of any tribe," I shouted back. It is his refusal of his birthright that makes him a poet and an individual worth respecting, I explained.

This wasn't true, of course. Many of the greatest poets in the history of the world have been fierce nationalists. The sole function of the epic poet is to find excuses for the butcheries of the innocent. In our big and comfy family bed today's murderers will sleep like little babies, is what they are always saying.

On the other side are the poets who trust only the solitary human voice. The lyric poet is almost by definition a traitor to his own people. He is the stranger who speaks the harsh truth that only individual lives are unique and therefore sacred. He may be loved by his people, but his example is also the one to be warned against. The tribe must pull together to face the invading enemy while the lyric poet sits talking to the skull in the graveyard.

For that reason he deserves to be exiled, put to death, and remembered.

> *Mistaken ideas always end in bloodshed, but in every case it is someone else's blood. This is why our thinkers feel free to say just about everything.*
>
> —Camus

"There are always a lot of people just waiting for a band wagon to jump on either for or against something," Hannah Arendt said in a letter. She knew what she was talking about. The terrifying thing about modern intellectuals everywhere is that they are always changing idols. At least religious fanatics stick mostly to what they believe in. All the rabid nationalists in Eastern Europe were Marxists yesterday and Stalinists last week. The freedom of the individual has never been their concern. They were after bigger fish. The sufferings of the world are an ideal chance for all intellectuals to have an experience of tragedy and to fulfill their utopian longings. If in the meantime one comes to share the views of some mass murderer, the end justifies the means. Modern tyrants have had some of the most illustrious literary salons.

Nationalism as much as Communism provides an opportunity to rewrite history. The problem with true history and great literature is that they wallow in ambiguities, unresolved issues, nuances, and baffling contradictions. Let's not kid ourselves. The Manichaean view of the world is much more satisfying. Any revision of history is acceptable providing it gives us some version of the struggle between angels and devils. If, in reality, this means dividing murderers in Yugoslavia into good and bad, so be it. If it means weeping from one eye at the death of a Moslem woman and winking from the other at the death of her Orthodox husband, that's the secret attraction of that model.

Our media, too, treat complexity the way Victorians treated sexuality—as something from which the viewer and the reader need to be protected. In the case of Yugoslavia, where nothing is simple, the consequences are more evil. Our columnists and intellectuals often have views identical to their nationalist counterparts in various parts of that country. In an age of PC, they miss hate and lynching mobs. The democratic forces in Yugoslavia can expect nothing from either side. At home they'll be treated as traitors and abroad their version of events will be greeted by silence for making the plot too complicated.

So what's to be done? people rightly ask. I've no idea. As an elegist I mourn and expect the worst. Vileness and stupidity always have a rosy future. The world is still a few evils short, but they'll come. Dark despair is the only healthy outlook if you identify yourself with the flies as I do. If, however, you secretly think of yourself as one of the spiders, or, God forbid, as the laughing philosopher himself, you have much less to worry about. Since you'll be on the winning side, you can always rewrite history and claim you were a fly. Elegies in a spider's web is all we bona fide flies get. That and the beauty of the sunrise like some unexpected touch of the executioner's final courtesy the day they take us out to be slaughtered. In the meantime, my hope is very modest. Let's have a true ceasefire for once, so the old lady can walk out into the rubble and find her cat.

Novica Tadić

The short poem is a wonder of nature. Epics grow unreadable, empires collapse, languages and cultures die, but there are short anonymous Egyptian poems, for instance, that have been around almost as long as the pyramids and are still full of life today.

The religion of the short poem, in every age and in every literature, has a single commandment: less is always more. The short poem rejects preamble and summary. It's about all and everything, the metaphysics of a few words surrounded by much silence.

"I'm sitting here wondering will a matchbox hold my clothes?" says an old blues song, and instantly the imagination starts working. We get the picture. The short poem is the poetic imagination in its essence, the epistemological ground of poetry and the place where the lyric is forever renewed.

> Jesus
> Our Jesus
> Our Jesus a pincushion

An image is worth a thousand words, we say. After a good one, one gasps for breath. There are images made with the eyes open and images made with the eyes closed. One is about clear sight and the other about similitude. In the best poems both come into play. The short poem is a match flaring up in a dark universe.

Written as an introduction to *Night Mail: Selected Poems of Novica Tadić*.

Whoever writes a short poem today inherits a long tradition. There are Sappho and Catullus, Arab albas and cassidas, Issa and Bashō, Imagist red wheelbarrows, and even Heraclitus and Pascal. The art of the short poem partakes of all kinds of brief jottings and utterances. For Tadić, there is, in addition, the Serbian folk tradition of riddles, proverbs, and magic incantations.

"A black flea guards my house," says a riddle. "Two magpies sit on the same bone and do not see each other," says another riddle, whose answer is "eyes." In this riddling world a nail goes to church so it can stand on its head, the calf in the field is like a king who dines while cracking his whip all around him.

"If not for the wind," the folk say, "the spiders would cover the sky with their webs. If they're suffering from yellow fever, they chant about a yellow rooster who flapped its yellow wings twice over a yellow hen on a yellow day of a yellow week of a yellow month of a yellow year."

And when it comes time to cuss, they say: "May a serpent drink from your eyes!"

In his scheme of things rats and mice running starved and terrified through the mazes heralded a new era.

—Kate Braverman

As with those great masters of the grotesque, Bosch and Goya, the world of Novica Tadić is distinct and immediately recognizable. We are in a city of loners, blind alleys, sewers, and unlit streets. Everywhere monsters lurk. We meet baby cyclops, giant hens, inanimate objects that make faces, and other fantastic crossbreeds. For Tadić reality is unstable, prone any moment to break into separate and unfamiliar pieces, only to suddenly reassemble itself. He is the poet who questions appearances and catalogues new species.

One thinks, of course, of medieval and Renaissance iconography. Some of Tadić's images could have come from illustrated books on black magic, alchemy, and witchcraft. They remind me also of the bibles of the Gnostics, fabulous bestiaries with their centaurs and winged sphinxes, Rabelais's grotesque exaggerations and diableries, the tales of Siberian shamans and tricksters, surrealist proverbs, diaries of lunatics, dreambooks of mystics, and the poems of the so-called "damned poets," Baudelaire, Lautréamont, and Rimbaud.

Tadić, too, is writing his season in hell. His hero is an anonymous city dweller, someone living in a mouse hole, or in some crack in the basement wall. The world is evil. Man was created in Satan's own image. It is the poetry of the new dark ages that Tadić writes. This is the natural history of a feverish brain full of dark premonitions at the end of a long and vile century. The world is making ugly faces back at us. The poet is the one who witnesses the constant metamorphosis of everything. The Demon of Analogy rules creation. An all-night freak show is in progress. The result is a kind of "grotesque realism," (Bakhtin's phrase), in which we recognize our historical nightmares in the terror of our solitude.

Bruno Schulz said: "The sublime nature of the divine order . . . can be rendered only by the power of human negation." He was speaking of Kafka's feel for the boundaries of the human and the divine. Tadić has the same feel. He composes anti-poems, anti-psalms, anti-prayers. He is Stevens's "metaphysician in the dark," a St. John of the Cross in a world in which only demons are left. What is astonishing about Tadić's accomplishment is that he has created a vision of such complexity in poems that are almost exclusively very short. In my view, he is one of the most original and interesting poets writing today.

Shop, Le Bacarès
Pyrénées-Orientales, France, 1950

*At the moment the writer realizes he has no ideas he has become
an artist.*

—Gilbert Sorrentino

A shop in a town of twisting streets. The hour of siesta and
immense heat. The street as empty as the Sahara.

"I didn't meet a soul," says the madman who walks in the
midday sun.

A greengrocer's shop with its sign almost faded. A shop
inviting reverie with its empty crates and baskets, its three
closed doors and black cat.

They were selling beans for cassoulet here while Napoleon
was retreating from Russia, dunking bread in the wine while
the Arabs were still in Spain.

How cool must be the leaves of young lettuce in the dark
shop with its low ceiling and thick walls! Are there baskets of
eggplants and peas still in their pods left unsold? I'm sure
there's an old-fashioned scale in there with its golden pans
balanced and empty in the half-darkness.

The one who feeds the cat is lying down in the upstairs
bedroom. She is a huge fat woman with enormous naked
arms and one eye open. She has heard steps.

The eye is wiser than the tongue even in the land of Des-
cartes and Mallarmé. "The eye has knowledge the mind can-
not share," says my friend Hayden Carruth. That knowledge
must have made the photographer stop.

What photography and modern poetry share is the belief

Written for a book of essays on the life and work of the photogra-
pher Paul Strand.

in the chance encounter. The image is presented without commentary—as in this old poem by William Carlos Williams, which Paul Strand, too, must have known.

> *Between Walls*
>
> the back wings
> of the
>
> hospital where
> nothing
>
> will grow lie
> cinders
>
> in which shine
> the broken
>
> pieces of a green
> bottle

The painter De Chirico says: "Then I had the strange impression that I was looking at these things for the first time and the composition of my picture came to my mind's eye. Now each time I look at this painting I again see the moment. Nevertheless, the moment is an enigma to me, for it is inexplicable. And I like also to call the work which sprang from it an enigma."

He is talking about familiar things restored to their strangeness, becoming, indeed, a school of metaphysics. The image is what we think about in its all-night classes.

It is not so much that all ages are contemporaneous, as Ezra Pound claimed, but that all the present moments certainly are. The trust in the present moment and the visible truth is what American poetry shares with photography. The present is the only place where we experience the eternal. The eternal shrinks to the size of the present because only the present is humanly graspable.

Peeling walls, a worn-out sign, nothing prosperous about the shop except for the balcony with its wrought iron railing and the finely carved heavy door. Did the house once belong to a rich merchant?

One must resist this temptation to "read" the photograph further and further, for its power lies precisely in its remaining always on the verge of being "read." With Baudelaire we say that a closed door is much more interesting than an open one.

Just then, as if on cue, a black cat came out to look at something to the side of the photographer.

The cat is the X in this equation. I expect never to get her out of my mind.

No Cure for the Blues

—Maurice Blanchot

A cold and windy day in New York City thirty years ago.
Outside an A&P market plastered with signs of that day's
specials, a beautiful old black man with a beat-up guitar, dark
glasses, tin cup, and an equally ancient seeing-eye dog lying at
his feet. He sings in high tenor voice:

> "Santi Claus, Santi Claus,
> Won't you please hear my lonesome plea.
> I don't want nothing for Christmas,
> But my baby back to me."

Later that day, crossing Central Park, I see a young woman
lying on a bench, her face hidden in her hands, her white
party dress just covering the backs of her knees, one of her
red shoes fallen off to the side. She is sleeping, or more likely
pretending to. In any case, I feel obliged to walk past her
almost on tiptoes.

No one else is around, and it's still cold and windy. I walk
briskly, looking back now and then, the last time when there's
no chance I can see her from so far away.

"Doing something wrong," sings Walter Davis.

> You show your linen to any man . . .
> You come home walking like a goose
> As if somebody turned you loose.

Written for a special issue of *Antaeus* on music and published in 1993.

The chief preoccupation of much country and urban blues is the relationship between men and women. Love, unfaithfulness, jealousy, hard times, good times, happy sex, bad sex, and everything else that keeps people awake tossing and turning at night, is the subject.

> You'll need me some morning when I won't need you.

Or,

> You've been a good ole wagon, Daddy,
> But you done broke down.

Or, there's the blues song Jelly Roll Morton claims is the first one he ever heard back in New Orleans in the early years of this century:

> Stood on the corner
> With her feet soaking wet,
> Begging each and every man
> That she met.
>
> If you can't give a dollar,
> Give me a lousy dime.
> I want to feed
> That hungry man of mine.

That's the blues at its most tragic. But the same Morton can also sing on another occasion:

> If you must go, sweet baby,
> Leave a dime for beer.

A kind of comic realism is at work in many of the songs, especially when the subject is love or sex. No wonder churchgoers called it devil's music. Everybody knows the devil likes to fool around. The comic seriousness of these songs understands the coexistence of misfortune and laughter. It is in that joyful irreverence and freedom that one must seek their truth.

Your nuts hang down like a damn bell clapper,
And your dick stands up like a steeple,
And your asshole stands open like a church door,
And crab walks in like people.

This is from the blues singer Lucille Bogan, who sang about sex with such abandon and humor that it seemed her purpose was to intentionally terrify the prudes. There was a commercial angle to it, of course. How else do you entertain a bunch of drunks in a dive? The critics who say sexual themes were forced on black performers are talking nonsense. I guess they were forced on poor Boccaccio and Rabelais, too. Money is not the whole explanation. There is poetry in some of that smut.

"I have something between my legs to make a dead man come," I overheard a woman once say to the young preacher at a wake which had turned boisterous with drink and good food. It was improper, but very funny, like this music, which knows only the truth of laughter and no inhibition.

They played blues records in Berlin in the 1920s. They heard "Jazzin' Babies Blues" on the banks of the Nile, "Mean Old Bedbug Blues" by the Yangtze River. I first heard the blues in Belgrade in 1947–48 when one could go to jail for listening to American music. We heard Louis Armstrong sing "St. James Infirmary." We lay on the floor next to the record player with the sound turned down low and the mother of my friend fretting in the next room.

Some people call me a hobo, some call me a bum,
Nobody knows my name, nobody knows what I've done.

Bessie Smith, Eva Taylor, Bertha Chippie Hill, Alberta Hunter, Sippie Wallace, Ada Brown, Ida Cox, Victoria Spivey—addicts of the blues know them all. I played Ethel Waters's "One Man Nan" till it hissed and skipped terribly. I could not play that record or most of my other records for anyone else. They would not understand my forbearance. At their best my records would sound like rain, a summer downpour in the city when everyone runs for cover, at their worst like a sausage patty being fried in a pan. It didn't matter. Sadness and happiness would well up in me with the first few notes. Why it it, I said to myself one night, that listening to the music I feel a homesickness for a vanished world that I was never a part of?

The blues prove the complete silliness of any theory of cultural separatism which denies the possibility of aesthetic experience outside one's race, ethnicity, religion, or even gender. Like all genuine art, the blues belong to a specific time, place, and people which it then, paradoxically, transcends. The secret of its transcendence lies in its minor key and its poetry of solitude. Lyric poetry has no closer relation anywhere than the blues. The reason people make lyric poems and blues songs is because our life is short, sweet, and fleeting. The blues bears witness to the strangeness of each individual's fate. It begins wordlessly in a moan, a stamp of the foot, a sigh, a hum, and then seeks words for that something or other that has no name in any language and for which all poetry and music seek an approximation.

The friendship of solitude, late night, and the blues. In 1959, I lived in a fleabag hotel in Greenwhich Village in a room no bigger than a closet and just as dark. There was a window, but it faced a brick wall. My nights were interrupted by creaking beds, smokers' coughs, and moans of love-making. I didn't sleep much. I lay in bed reading, chain-smoking, and drinking wine. I had a radio and a cheap portable record player.

> Nobody loves me but my mother,
> And she could be jiving too.

Some old sage claims that the soul is made between one or two in the morning. I agree, especially if you're listening to the blues. I owned a few records, but it was the radio that brought me surprises and delights from time to time. Playing with the dial, I'd come across an unknown voice, a cornet, and a piano that would make me turn up the volume in my excitement. I lay with eyes closed, astonished that such a fine song existed and regretting already that it would end. Very often the D.J. would not even name the performer, and what I'd heard would haunt me for years, until in my manic record-buying I would come upon that very cut.

One night I was listening to a program devoted to Leroy Carr and Scrapper Blackwell, that great piano-and-guitar duo that made so many records back in the 1930s, when there was a soft knock on the door. It was a quarter to three. I thought somebody had complained to the night clerk about me, but why was he knocking so softly? I didn't budge. Carr could have been singing something like:

> Ain't it lonesome
> Sleeping by yourself
> When the woman that you love
> Is loving someone else?

Finally, I opened the door a crack. Outside, an old man stood as if shivering in his T-shirt, pants, and with nothing on his feet. "What's that beautiful music?" he asked me with a heavy Italian accent. I told him. Carr went on singing, so I let him in. He sat in my only chair and I sat on the bed.

> In the wee midnight hour
> Long before the break of day,
> When the blues creep upon you
> And carry your mind away.

My visitor listened with a serious, even pious expression. He didn't say much, except to call the music nice, very nice, much too nice. We parted when the program was over, and I never saw him again.

> Some people tell me,
> God takes care of old folks and fools,
> But since I've been born,
> He must've changed the rules.

The guitar player who sang this recorded, under the name Funny Papa Smith, some twenty sides between 1930–31.

They say he wore a stovepipe hat and work-overalls, but not in the picture I have of him, where he wears a suit, bow tie, and the kind of hat a traveling salesman might wear. A good-looking young fellow with a sensitive, even melancholy, expression. I can well believe he was a gambler, but I'm surprised to learn that he murdered a man. I read someplace that he ended up in the electric chair, but I've no idea if this is true. All I know is that he sang an astonishing two-part hoodoo blues called "Seven Sisters."

> They tell me Seven Sisters in New Orleans, that can really fix
>   a man up right,
> And I'm headed for New Orleans, Louisiana, I'm traveling
>   both day and night.
> I hear them say the oldest sister look like she's just twenty-one
> And said she can look right in your eyes and tell you exactly
>   what you want done.
> They tell me they been hung, been bled and been crucified
> But I just want enough help to stand on the water and rule
>   the tide.
> It's bound to be Seven Sisters 'cause I've heard it by
>   everybody else.
> 'Course I'd love to take their word, but I'd rather go and see
>   for myself.
> When I leave the Seven Sisters I'm piling stones all around
> And go to my baby and tell her there's another Seven-Sister
>   man in town.
> Good mornin' Seven Sisters, just thought I'd come down and
>   see
> Will you build me up where I'm torn down and make me
>   strong where I'm weak?
> I went to New Orleans, Louisiana, just on account of
>   something I heard.
> The Seven Sisters told me everything I wanted to know and
>   they wouldn't let me speak a word.
> Now it's Sara, Minnie, Bertha, Holly, Dolly, Betty and Jane—
> You can't know them sisters apart because they all looks just
>   the same
> The Seven Sisters sent me away happy, 'round the corner I
>   met another little girl;
> She looked at me and smiled and said: Go devil and destroy
>   the world.

[Spoken: I'm gonna destroy it, too . . . I'm all right now]
Seven times you hear the Seven Sisters, will visit me in my
   sleep,
And they said I won't have no more trouble, and said I'll live
   twelve days in a week.
Boy go down in Louisiana, and get the lead right outta your
   being.
If Seven Sisters can't do anything in Louisiana, bet you'll have
   to go to New Orleans.

Small masterpieces by nearly unknown performers are the rule when it comes to the history of recorded blues. Again, it must have been the usual makeshift recording studio in some hotel room on a street of pool halls, whorehouses, and dance halls. The year was 1931. Around the corner, probably, there was a soup kitchen with a line of unemployed black men and, inside, a straight-backed chair and a bottle of whiskey for the musician.

There was nothing customary about what Smith sang. Here was a blues song about the secret world of voodoo, eroticism, crime, and god-knows-what-else, in a lingo both poetic and obscure. In this blues, as in many others, one glimpses an unknown America with an imagination and imagery all its own. The blues poet has been where we are all afraid to go, as if there was a physical place, a forbidden place that corresponds to a place in ourselves where we experience the tragic sense of life and its amazing wonders. In that dive, in that all-night blues and soul club, we feel the full weight of our fate, we taste the nothingness at the heart of our being, we are simultaneously wretched and happy, we spit on it all, we want to weep and raise hell, because the blues, in the end, is about a sadness older than the world, and there's no cure for that.

Poetry Is the Present

Throughout his life Octavio Paz has remained free, tempted by neither the ideological utopias nor the nostalgia that has proliferated and imprisoned so many of his contemporaries. Someone—I forgot who—said that it takes a heroic constitution to endure our modern age. Paz is one of our true heroes. In times of the celebrated incommunicability of just about everything, he has thought and written with clarity. He has understood what he knows—which again makes him unusual.

I would characterize his thinking as the most sustained, the most eloquent defense of poetry that we have.

Does poetry need to be defended? Of course. Always—and especially today.

Last night Octavio Paz told us, "Poetry is the present." I couldn't agree more. This is poetry's most outrageous idea, and it has a long and interesting history, of which I wish to speak briefly.

We are not sure who was first, Sappho or some forgotten contemporary of hers, but in the seventh century b.c. we hear something new in poetry, a voice in solitude for which the present moment is everything:

> The moon and Pleiades are set,
> the night is half gone
> and time speeds by.
> I lie in bed, alone.

Delivered as a lecture at a conference on Octavio Paz and published in *Western Humanities Review* in 1991.

Before that, of course, there was the epic, with its clashing swords, its stories of gods and heroes, and many other kinds of poems, but nothing that sounds quite like Sappho. In another poem she says:

> I remember Anaktoria
> who has gone from me
> and whose lovely walk and the shining pallor
> of her face I would rather see before my
> eyes than Lydia's chariots in all their glory
> armored for battle.

All of a sudden, instead of the stories of gods and heroes, we get the lives of the poets. In other words, not what Zeus and Achilles did but what some woman on an island off Asia Minor felt on a particular night when she couldn't sleep. Her voice, her life, her timeless moment resonate through the centuries.

The lyric poem represents a great change in the history of consciousness and the history of literature. Olga Friedenberg observed that it marks a shift from a mythologized to a realistic view of the world. It is in lyric poetry that the literary universe is inhabited for the first time by individuals. There were always lyric poems, folksongs sung by women, but their speaker was anonymous. Sappho inserts the first-person pronoun, makes the experience of the folksong personal. It is women who invented the lyric poem.

The philosophers and theologians were scandalized. The early Christian Church burned the writings of Sappho with fanatical thoroughness. Today only fragments of her poems are left. About her life we know next to nothing. Some ancient authors say she was a priestess, some say a prostitute.

It's curious that in our century the same words occur in the condemnation of the Russian poetess, Anna Akhmatova. Stalin's cultural czar, Andrey Zhdanov, said, here's a little bourgeois lady, half-nun, half-whore. He said that her intensely personal poems with their mixture of eroticism and mysticism were foreign to the spirit of the Soviet people, who were building socialism.

"O consciousness, pure present where past and future

burn with neither brilliance nor hope. Everything leads into this eternity which leads nowhere," writes Paz in a poem.

Poetry is the moment, the experience of the naked moment. It's not so much that all ages are contemporaneous, as Ezra Pound claimed, but that all present moments in literature are.

There's more to this than that, however. The proposition that "poetry is the present" has philosophical ambitions which the ancient philosophers and theologians already suspected and twentieth-century Marxists severely punished.

This is what lyric poets are saying: While philosophy and theology ask what Being is, poetry gives us the experience of Being. The poets, so we believe, remind the philosophers, again and again, of the world's baffling presence.

Unfortunately, not many contemporary philosophers and literary critics believe any of this. As Hayden Carruth once told me, "We poets of the second half of the twentieth century are really displaced metaphysicians of the nineteenth century, people still living in the regions of thought that the philosophers have fled out of bafflement and despair and false modesty." He's right, of course. As far as some people are concerned, poetry is just whistling in the dark.

"There's no presence," says our distinguished critic, Geoffrey Hartman, "there's only representation, and worse, representations." "There's nothing outside the text," says Jacques Derrida. Poets, they claim, share in the bourgeois notion that signs are transparent, that they point to an authentic reality. "A seductive temptation to mystified minds," Paul de Man assures us.

The truth-value of poetry, therefore, is zero. All the poets' images and metaphors merely point back to language itself, we are told triumphantly. Plato imprisoned us in a cave to demonstrate our ignorance and the terror of our situation, but in today's prisonhouse of language our philosophers are happy.

Language is not the only prison. We are incarcerated, so they say, in prisons of class, race, gender, culture, and so on. Today's intellectual landscape is that of prisons, maximum-security penitentiaries, and philosophical gulags.

Such notions sound plausible if we forget many things about literature, and especially if we forget translation. How is it that we find ancient Greek poetry moving if there are no universal experiences? As my friend Mark Strand and I realized years ago, poetry is not what is lost but what is retained in translation.

I agree with Paz that it is impossible to be a poet without believing in the identity of the word and what it means. There's that something beyond language on which every poem depends for its existence. The complaint that language pretends to make things present to us but always fails to do so is no news to poets. Yes, writing does distort presence. Yes, there's an abyss between the words and the experience of presence the poem is trying to name. Yet we still have a pretty good idea what Sappho and Akhmatova are saying.

"In the moment of time when the small drop forms, but does not fall," says Theodore Roethke. American poetry has been obsessed with presence and visible truth since the days of Emerson and Whitman. "By visible truth we mean the apprehension of the absolute condition of present things," writes Melville to Hawthorne in a letter. The subject of much American poetry is the epistemology of presence. Frost, Stevens, and Williams all have something to say about that. John Ashbery's magnificent poem "Self-Portrait in a Convex Mirror" is a meditation on that enigma, "that stranger," as he calls it, "the mute, undivided present."

"To unlock the instant, to / penetrate its astonished rooms . . ." (again Paz). Here's a point at which time and eternity, history and consciousness meet, a fragment of time haunted by the whole of time. The present is the only place where we experience the eternal. The eternal shrinks to the size of the present because only the present can be humanly grasped.

In its essence a lyric poem is about time stopped. Language moves in time, but the lyric impulse is vertical. Of course, one can't really say what presence is; one can only attempt to say what it is like. Sometimes—and this is a paradox—only wildest imaginings can bridge the abyss of word and thing.

Poetry thrives on such contradictions. One is both using language and being used by language, for instance. I love Sappho's sense of the moment, but I also have Homer's one-eyed giants, many-headed monsters, not to mention those women who are half fish and who sing so beautifully that sailors have to stick wax in their ears or they go nuts, plus all his other wonderful inventions. The best thing about poetry is that it greatly upsets schoolmasters, preachers, and dictators, and cheers up the rest of us.

The Necessity of Poetry

Late night on MacDougal Street. An old fellow comes up to me and says: "Sir, I'm writing the book of my life and I need a dime to complete it." I give him a dollar.

Another night in Washington Square Park, a fat woman with fright wig says to me: "I'm Esther, the goddess of Love. If you don't give me a dollar, I'll put a curse on you." I give her a nickel.

One of those postwar memories: a baby carriage pushed by a humpbacked old woman, her son sitting in it, both legs amputated.

She was haggling with the greengrocer when the carriage got away from her. The street was steep so it rolled downhill with the cripple waving his crutch, his mother screaming for help, and everybody else laughing as if they were in the movies. Buster Keaton or somebody like that about to go over a cliff . . .

One laughed because one knew it would end well. One was surprised when it didn't.

I didn't tell you how I got lice wearing a German helmet. This used to be a famous story in our family. I remember those winter evenings just after the war with everybody huddled around the stove, talking and worrying late into the night.

These memoir fragments were written between 1987 and 1993.

Sooner or later, it was inevitable, somebody would bring up my German helmet full of lice. They thought it was the funniest thing they ever heard. Old people had tears of laughter in their eyes. A kid dumb enough to walk around with a German helmet full of lice. They were crawling all over it. Any fool could see them!

I sat there saying nothing, pretending to be equally amused, nodding my head while thinking to myself, what a bunch of idiots! All of them! They had no idea how I got the helmet, and I wasn't about to tell them.

It was in those first days just after the liberation of Belgrade, I was up in the old cemetery with a few friends, kind of snooping around. Then, all of a sudden, we saw them! A couple of German soldiers, obviously dead, stretched out on the ground. We drew closer to take a better look. They had no weapons. Their boots were gone, but there was a helmet that had fallen to the side of one of them. I don't remember what the others got, but I went for the helmet. I tiptoed so as not to wake the dead man. I also kept my eyes averted. I never saw his face, even if sometimes I think I did. Everything else about that moment is still intensely clear to me.

That's the story of the helmet full of lice.

Beneath the swarm of high-flying planes we were eating watermelon. While we ate the bombs fell on Belgrade. We watched the smoke rise in the distance. We were hot in the garden and asked to take our shirts off. The watermelon made a ripe, cracking noise as my mother cut it with a big knife. We also heard what we thought was thunder, but when we looked up, the sky was cloudless and blue.

My mother heard a man plead for his life once. She remembers the stars, the dark shapes of trees along the road on which they were fleeing the Austrian army in a slow-moving ox-cart. "That man sounded terribly frightened out there in the woods," she says. The cart went on. No one said anything. Soon they could hear the river they were supposed to cross.

In my childhood women mended stockings in the evening. To have a "run" in one's stocking was catastrophic. Stockings were expensive, and so was electricity. We would all sit around the table with a single lamp, my grandmother reading the papers, we children pretending to do our homework, while watching my mother spreading her red-painted fingernails inside the transparent stocking.

In the biography of the Russian poet, Marina Tsvetaeva, I read that her first poetry reading in Paris took place on February 6, 1925, and the newspaper announcement says that there were also three musicians on the program, Madame Cunelli, who sang old Italian songs, Professor Mogilewski, who played violin, and V. E. Byutsov, who was on piano. This was astonishing! Madame Cunelli, whose first name was Nina, was a friend of my mother's. They both studied with the same voice teacher, Madame Kedrov, in Paris, and then somehow Nina Cunelli ended up in Belgrade during the Second World War where she taught me Russian and French children's songs, which I still know well. I remember that she was a beautiful woman, a little older than my mother, and that she went abroad after the war ended.

There was a maid in our house who let me put my hand under her skirt. I was five or six years old. I can still remember the dampness of her crotch and my surprise that there was all that hair there. I couldn't get enough of it. She would crawl under the table where I had my military fort and my toy soldiers. I don't remember what was said, if anything. Just her hand, firmly guiding mine to that spot.

They sit on the table, the tailors do. At least, they used to. A street of dim shops in Belgrade where we went to have my father's coat narrowed and shortened so it would fit me. The tailor got off the table and stuck pins in my shoulder. "Don't squirm," my mother said. Outside it was getting dark. Large snowflakes fell.

Years later in New York, on the same kind of afternoon, a dry-cleaning store window with an ugly, thick-legged woman on the chair in a white dress. She's having the hems raised by a gray-headed Jewish tailor, who kneels before her as if he is proposing marriage.

There was an expensive-looking suitcase on the railroad tracks, and they were afraid to come near it. Far from any station, on a stretch of track bordered by orchards where they had been stealing plums that afternoon. The suitcase, she remembers, had colorful labels, of what were probably world-famous hotels and ocean liners. During the war, of course, one heard of bombs, special ones, in the shape of toys, pens, soccer balls, exotic birds—so why not suitcases? For that reason they left it where it was.

"I always wondered what was in it," my wife says. We were talking about the summer of 1944, of which we both had only a few clear recollections.

The world was going up in flames and I was studying violin. The baby Nero sawing away . . .

My teacher's apartment was always cold. A large, almost empty room with a high ceiling already in shadow. I remember the first few screechy notes my violin would make and my teacher's stern words of reprimand. I was terrified of that old woman. I also loved her because after the scolding she would give me something to eat. Something rare and exotic, like chocolate filled with sweet liqueur. We'd sit in that big empty room, almost dark now. I'd be eating and she'd be watching me eat. "Poor child," she'd say, and I thought it had to do with my not practicing enough, my being dim-witted when she tried to explain something to me, but today I'm not sure that's what she meant. In fact, I suspect she had something else entirely in mind. That's why I am writing this, to find out what it was.

When my grandfather was dying from diabetes, when he had already had one leg cut off at the knee and they were threatening to do the same to the other, his old buddy, Savo Lozanic, used to visit him every morning to keep him company. They would reminisce about this and that and even have a few laughs.

One morning my grandmother had to leave him alone in the house, as she had to attend the funeral of a distant relative. That's what gave him the idea. He hopped out of bed and into the kitchen, where he found candles and matches. He got back into his bed, somehow placed one candle above his head and the other at his feet, and lit them. Finally, he pulled the sheet over his face and began to wait.

When his friend knocked, there was no answer. The door being unlocked, he went in, calling from time to time. The kitchen was empty. A fat gray cat slept on the dining room table. When he entered the bedroom and saw the bed with the sheet and lit candles, he let out a wail and then broke into sobs as he groped for a chair to sit down.

"Shut up, Savo," my grandfather said sternly from under his sheet. "Can't you see I'm only practicing?"

I leave the dentist's chair after what seems an eternity. It's an evening in June. I'm walking the tree-lined streets full of dark, whispering trees in my neighborhood in Belgrade. The streets are poorly lit, but there are people about strolling close to each other as if they were lovers. The thought crosses my mind that this is the happiest moment in my life.

In Chicago, in the 1950s, there was still an old woman with a street organ and a monkey. She turned the crank with both hands while the monkey went around with a tin cup. It was some vaguely familiar tune that made our grandmothers sigh in their youth.

The woman looked like she must've known the cow that started the Great Fire. Later she married an Italian with a street organ. At times he kissed her with the monkey still on his shoulder.

The animal I saw looked young and full of mischief. He wore a tattered coat with brass buttons, which he must have inherited from his father. That day they had for an audience a small boy who wanted one of the monkey's bells. His beautiful mother kept pulling his arm to go, but he wouldn't budge. The old woman turning the crank had her eyes raised to heaven in a manner favored by saints who are being tempted by demons.

Another story about time. This one about the time it took them to quit their cells after beginning to suspect that the Germans were gone. In that huge prison in Milan all of a sudden you could hear a pin drop. Eventually they thought it best to remove their shoes before walking out.

My father was still tiptoeing hours later crossing a large empty piazza. There was a full moon above the dark palaces. His heart was in his mouth.

"It was just like an opera stage," he says. "All lit up, but nobody in the audience, and nobody in the orchestra pit. Nevertheless, I felt like singing. Or perhaps screaming?"

He did neither. The year was 1944.

The streets are empty, it's raining, and we are sitting in the Hotel Sherman bar listening to the bluesy piano. I'm not yet old enough to order a drink, but my father's presence is so authoritative and intimidating that when he orders for me the waiters never dare to ask about my age.

We talk. My father remembers a fly that wouldn't let him sleep one summer afternoon fifty years ago. I tell him about an old gray overcoat twice my size, which my mother made me wear after the war. It was wintertime. People on the street would sometimes stop and watch me. The overcoat trailed the ground and made walking difficult. One day I was standing on the corner waiting to cross when a young woman gave me a small coin and walked away. I was so embarrassed.

"Was she pretty?" my father asks.

"Not at all," I tell him. She looked like a hick, maybe a nun.

"A Serbian Ophelia," my father thinks.

It's possible. Anything is possible.

The huge crowd cheering the dictator; the smiling faces of children offering flowers in welcome. How many times have I seen that? And always the same blonde little girl curtsying! Here she is surrounded by the high boots of the dignitaries and a couple of tightly leashed police dogs. The monster himself is patting her on the head and whispering in her ear.

I look in vain for someone with a troubled face.

The exiled general's grandson was playing war with his cheeks puffed to imitate bombs exploding. The grim daughter wrote down the old man's reminiscences. The whole apartment smelled of bad cooking.

The general was in a wheelchair. He wore a bib and smoked a cigar. The daughter smiled for me and my mother in a way that made her sharp little teeth show.

I like the general better. He remembered some prime minister pretending to wipe his ass with a treaty he had just signed, the captured enemy officers drinking heavily and toasting some cabaret singer form their youth.

It's your birthday. The child you were appears on the street wearing a stupid grin. He wants to take you by the hand, but you won't let him.

"You've forgotten something," he whispers. And you, quiet as a mutt around an undertaker, since, of course, he (the child) doesn't exist.

There was an old fellow at the *Sun Times,* who was boss when I first came and worked as a mail clerk, who claimed to have read everything. His father was a janitor at the university library in Urbana, and Stanley, for that was his name, started as a kid. At first I didn't believe any of it; then I asked him about Gide, whom I was then reading. He recited for me the names of the major novels and their plots. What about Isaac Babel, Alain Fournier, Aldous Huxley, Ford Madox Ford? The same thing. It was amazing! Everything I had read or heard of he had already read. You should be on a quiz show, Stanley, people who overheard us said. Stanley had never been to college and had worked for the papers most of his life. He had a stutter, so I guess that explains why he never married or got ahead. So, all he did was read books. I had the impression that he loved every book he read. Only superlatives for Stanley, one book better than the other. If I started to criticize, he'd get pissed off. Who do I think I am? Smartass, he called me, and wouldn't talk to me about books for a few days. Stanley was pure enthusiasm. I was giddy myself at the thought of another book waiting for me to read at home.

In Chicago there was a tremendous suspicion of the Eastern literary establishment. The working people never get portrayed in their books, I heard people say all the time. Most of the people I met were leftist intellectuals from working-class and immigrant backgrounds. These were Jews, Poles, Germans, Irish. They had relatives who worked in factories. They knew America could be a cruel place, an unjust country. After I saw South Chicago and Gary, Indiana, I had to admit they had a point. Both places, with their steel mills in smoke and fire, were like hell out of Hieronymus Bosch. The ugliness and poverty of industrial Chicago was an enormous influence on me. It prevented me from forgetting where I came from. A big temptation for all immigrants with intellectual pretensions is to outdo the natives in their love of Henry James and whatever he represents. You want to blend in, so you're always looking for role models. It's very understandable. Who wants to look and talk like a foreigner forever!

The night of my farewell dinner in Chicago, I got very drunk. At some point, I went to the bathroom and could not find my way back. The restaurant was large and full of mirrors. I would see my friends seated in the distance, but when I hurried toward them, I would come face to face with myself in a mirror. With my new beard I did not recognize myself immediately and almost apologized. In the end, I gave up and sat at an old man's table. He ate in silence, and I lit a cigarette. Time passed. The place was emptying. The old man finally wiped his mouth and pushed his full, untouched wine glass toward me. I would have stayed with him indefinitely if one of the women from our party hadn't found me and led me outside.

Did I lie a little? Of course. I gave the impression that I had lived for years on the Left Bank and often sat at the tables of the famous cafés watching the existentialists in their passionate arguments. What justified these exaggerations in my eyes was the real possibility that I could have done something like that. Everything about my life already seemed a fluke, a series of improbable turns of events, so in my case fiction was no stranger than truth. Like when I told the woman on the train from Chicago that I was a Russian. I described our apartment in Leningrad, the terrors of the long siege during the War, the deaths of my parents before a German firing squad which we children had to witness, the DP camps in Europe. At some point during the long night I had to go to the bathroom and simply laugh.

How much of it did she believe? Who knows? In the morning she gave me a long kiss in parting, which could have meant anything.

My father and his best friend talking about how some people resemble animals. The birdlike wife of so and so, for example. The many breeds of dogs and their human look-alikes. The lady who is a cow. The widow next door who is a tigress, etc.

"And what about me?" says my father's friend.

"You look like a rat, Tony," he replies without a moment's hesitation, after which they just sit drinking without saying another word.

"You look like a young Franz Schubert," the intense-looking woman told me as we were introduced.

At that same party, I spoke to a lawyer who insisted we had met in London two years before. I explained my accent to a doctor by telling him that I was raised by a family of deaf mutes.

There was a girl there, too, who kept smiling sweetly at me without saying anything. Her mother told me that I reminded her of her brother, who was executed by the Germans in Norway. She was going to give me more details, but I excused myself, telling everyone that I had a sudden and terrible toothache that required immediate attention.

I got the idea of sleeping on the roof in Manhattan on hot nights from my mother and father. That's what they did during the War, except it wasn't a roof but a large terrace on the top floor of a building in downtown Belgrade. There was a blackout, of course. I remember immense starry skies, and how silent the city was. I would begin to speak, but someone— I could not tell for a moment who it was—would put a hand over my mouth.

Like a ship at sea we were with stars and clouds up above. We were sailing full speed ahead. "That's where the infinite begins," I remember my father pointing with his long, dark hand.

If my father has a ghost, he's standing outside some elegant men's store on Madison Avenue on a late summer evening. A tall man studying a pair of brown suede Italian shoes. He himself is impeccably dressed in a tan suit, a blue shirt of an almost purple hue with a silk tie the color of rusty rose. He seems in no hurry. At the age of fifty-three, with his hair thinning and slicked back, he could be an Italian or a South American. Belle Georgio, one waitress in Chicago used to call him. No one would guess by his appearance that he is almost always broke.

I'm packing parcels in the Lord & Taylor basement during the Christmas rush with a bunch of losers. One fellow is an inventor. He has a new kind of aquarium with piped music, which makes it look as if the fish are doing water ballet, but the world is not interested. Another man supports three ex-wives, so he has a night job in addition to this one. His eyes close all the time. He's so pale, he could pass for a stiff in an open coffin.

Then there's Felix, a mousy fellow a bit older than I who claims to be a distant relative of the English royal family. One time he brought the chart of his family tree to make us stop laughing and explained the connection. What did not make sense is his poverty. He said he was a writer but wouldn't tell us what kind. "Are you writing porno?" one Puerto Rican girl asked him.

Her name was Rosie. She liked boxing. One time she and I went on a date to watch the fights at the Garden. We sat in the Spanish section. "Kill him! Kill him!" she screamed all evening without interruption. At the end she was so tired she wouldn't even have a drink with me, and had to rush home.

At a poetry reading given by Allen Tate I met a young poet who was attending a workshop given by Louise Bogan at NYU. I sat in a few times and accompanied my new friends for beers after class. One day I even showed two of my poems to Bogan. One was called "Red Armchair," and it had to do with an old chair thrown out on the sidewalk for the trashmen to pick up. The other poem I don't remember. Bogan was very kind. She fixed a few things but was generally encouraging, which surprised me, since I didn't think much of the poems myself.

The other critique of my poetry came later that fall and it was devastating. I had met a painter in a bar, an older fellow living in poverty with a wife and two small kids in a cold water flat in the Village, where he painted huge, realistic canvases of derelicts in the manner of 1930s socialist realism. A skyscraper and underneath a poor man begging. The message was obvious, but the colors were nice.

Despite the difference in our ages, we saw each other quite a bit, talking art and literature, until one day I showed him my poems. We were sitting in his kitchen with a bottle of whiskey between us. He leaned back in the chair and read the poems slowly, slowly while I watched him closely. At some point I began to detect annoyance in him and then anger. Finally, he looked at me as if seeing me for the first time and said something like: "Simic, I thought you were a smart kid. This is pure shit you're writing!"

I was prepared for gentle criticism in the manner of Louise Bogan, even welcomed it, but his bluntness stunned me. I left in a daze. I was convinced he was right. If I'd had a pistol, I would have shot myself on the spot. Then, little by little, mulling over what he had said, I got pissed off. There were some good things in my poems, I thought. "Fuck him," I shouted to some guy who came my way in the street. Of course, he was right, too, and it hurt me that he was, but all the same.

I came out of my daze just I was entering Central Park on 59th Street. I had walked more than sixty blocks totally oblivious of my surroundings. I sat on a bench and reread my poems, crossing out most of the lines, attempting to rewrite them then and there, still angry, still miserable, and at the same time grimly determined.

There was this old guy in Washington Square Park who used to lecture me about Sacco and Vanzetti and the great injustice done to them. We'd share a bench from time to time, and I'd hear him say again and again how if shit was worth money the poor would be born without assholes. He wore gray gloves, walked with a cane, tipped his hat to ladies, and worried about me. "A kid just off the boat," he'd say to someone passing by. "Sure to get screwed if he doesn't watch out."

I went to see Ionesco's *Bald Soprano* with Boris. It was being presented at the small theater in the Village. There were only six people in the audience, and that included the two of us. They gave the performance anyway. When it came to the love scene with the woman who has three noses, the actors got carried away on the couch. Their voices went down to a whisper as they started undressing each other. Boris and I just looked at each other. The other four people had suddenly become invisible. Well, they didn't fuck each other, but they came very close. I have no recollection of the rest of the play except that at the exit the streets were covered with newly fallen snow.

I was five minutes late from lunch at the insurance company where I was working and my boss chewed me out for being irresponsible in front of twenty or thirty other drudges. I sat at my desk for a while fuming, then I rose slowly, wrapped my scarf around my neck and put my gloves on in plain view of everybody, and walked out without looking back. I didn't have an overcoat and on the street it was snowing, but I felt giddy, deliriously happy at being free.

"My boy seeks the secret and the meaning of Time," we are told upon entering. If we weren't told, we'd say he's just staring out of the window at the rain. His mother wants us to be very quiet as we inspect the room she's thinking of renting.

"Povera e nuda via, Filosofia," wrote the Italian poet Petrarch. The rain getting heavier and then the sound of thunder over Manhattan.

The face of my daughter lit by a table lamp while she sucks a finger pricked by a compass, a drop of blood already fallen on the black letters and numerals of the difficult homework, as she worries whether to hand it in, just as it is, to the stern old nun who'll make her stand in front of the class waiting for the verdict . . . The spring day bright with sunlight. The nun's small, tight fist clouding the answer.

We were on our third bottle of wine when he said he was going to show me the pictures of his girlfriend. To my surprise, the photographs spread out on the table were of a naked woman shamelessly displaying herself. Leaning over my shoulder, he wanted me to note each detail, her crotch, her ass, her breasts, until I felt aroused. It was an odd situation. My host's pregnant wife was asleep in the next room. The photographs were spread all over the dining room table. There must've been close to a hundred of them. I looked and I listened. From time to time, I could hear the wife snore.

Approaching Manhattan on the train at night, I remember the old Polish and Ukrainian women wielding their mops in the brightly lit towers. I'd be working on some ledger that wouldn't balance, and they'd be scrubbing floors on their knees. They were fat and they all wore flowered dresses. The youngest would stand on a chair and dust off the portrait of the grim founder of the company. The old black man who ran the elevator would bow to them like a headwaiter in a fancy restaurant as he took them from one floor to the next. That would make them laugh. You'd see they had teeth missing. More than a few teeth missing.

It was a window with a view of a large office with many identical desks at which men and women sat working. A woman got up with papers in hand and walked the length of the floor to where a man rose to meet her at the other end. He waved his arms as he talked, while she stood before him with her head lowered, and I went on tying my necktie in the hotel room across the street. I was about to turn away from the window when I realized that the man was yelling at the woman, and that she was sobbing.

Here's a scene for you. My father and I are walking down Madison, when I spot a blue overcoat in a store called the

British American House. We study it, comment on the cut, and my father suggests I try it on. I know he has no money, but he insists since it's beginning to snow a little and I'm only wearing a tweed jacket. We go in, I put it on, and it fits perfectly. Immediately, I'm in love with it. We ask the price and it's two hundred dollars—which was a lot of money in 1959. Too bad, I think, but then my father asks me if I want it. I think maybe he's showing off in front of the salesman or he's come into some money he hasn't told me about. Do you want it? he asks again while the salesman goes to attend to another customer. You've no money George, I remind him, expecting him to contradict me or come to his senses. "Don't worry," is his reply.

I've seen him do this before and it embarrasses me. He asks for the boss and the two of them sequester themselves for a while, while I stand around waiting for us to be kicked out. Instead, he emerges triumphant and I wear the overcoat into the street. A born con man. His manner and appearance inspired such confidence that with a small downpayment and promise to pay the rest in a week or two, he'd get what he wanted. This was in the days before credit cards and credit bureaus when store owners had to make such decisions on the spot. They trusted him, and he did pay eventually whatever he owed. The crazy thing was that he pulled this stunt only in the best stores. It would never occur to him to ask for credit from a grocer, and yet he often went hungry despite his huge salary.

My father had phenomenal debts. He borrowed money any chance he had and paid his bills only when absolutely necessary. It was nothing for him to spend the rent money the night before it was due. I lived in terror of my landlords and landladies while he seemingly never worried. We'd meet after work and he'd suggest dinner in a French restaurant and I'd resist knowing it was his rent money he was proposing to spend. He'd describe the dishes and wines we could have in tantalizing detail, and I'd keep reminding him of the rent. He'd explain to me slowly, painstakingly, as if I were feeble-minded, that one should never worry about the future. We'll never be so young as we are tonight, he'd say. If we are smart, and we are, tomorrow we'll figure out how to pay the rent. In the end, who could say no? I never did.

On the street corner the card trickster was shuffling his three cards using a large cardboard box as a table. The cards, the quick hands fluttered. It looked like a cock fight. Five of us watching without expression, our heads, in the meantime, buzzing with calculations and visions of riches. The day was cold so we all had to squint.

Tough guys, he said, time to place your bets.

I became more and more lucid the later it got. This was always my curse. Everybody was already asleep. I tried to wake my dearest, but she drew me down on her breasts sleepily. We made love, slowly, languidly, and then I talked to her for hours about the necessity of poetry while she slept soundly.

Luneville Diary
(December 1, 1962–March 1, 1963)

We just sit around in our underwear listening to the radio and playing cards. There are four of us. The sergeant has a room of his own on the other side of the kitchen. Now that the weather has turned bad, there is not much police duty. The bus for Luneville leaves at six every evening, but there's hardly anybody on it. Our schedule is very simple. Two of us work every night and don't go patrolling before ten. The patrol drives to Luneville, has a drink at the train station café, checks a few bars frequented by GI's, makes sure everybody is on the 11:30 bus, and concludes the evening with a couple more drinks at the station. On Saturday nights there are a few more soldiers in bars since the curfew is not till one, but so far there have not been any serious incidents. The police radio is silent. The only time we use it is to ask the patrol on duty to bring back some sandwiches from the train station. We no longer eat in the mess hall. The last time was at Thanksgiving. We all dressed nice in our civvies and strolled over there. We got nothing but dirty looks. Besides, the baked potatoes and the turkey were raw. We never went back. We buy food in St. Clement or eat in its only café. Even the redneck Edwards is beginning to discriminate between different kinds of pâté.

This essay was published in *Gettysburg Review* in 1993.

The weather in eastern France is awful. In the summer it rains all the time and in the winter it snows when it's not raining. In the month that I've been here, we haven't had a single clear day. It would be very depressing except for the life we are leading. At Toul, there were morning formations, alerts, extra duty, inspections. Here we don't even hang our clothes in our lockers. We just throw everything on the floor. Sgt. Briggs doesn't give a shit. He's in love with a waitress in Luneville and dreams of taking her back to South Dakota. When they have a fight, which is often, I write letters of apology for him in terrible French. It seems she doesn't speak any English and has two little kids. That's all we know.

He's gone a lot during the day. Since there are five of us including the sergeant, we divide our working time this way: two on duty, two on standby, and one off over a twenty-four-hour period. What this means is that nobody works very hard. "We got it made," PFC Williams keeps reminding us. This is what life ought to be, according to him. When he gets back to LA, he's going to open a high-class whorehouse. Then he'll really have it made, he tells us. We think he's kidding about the whorehouse, but he's not. "The best Mexican pussy north of the border at popular American prices." Anytime we are in California we can get it free. We go to bed every night thinking of that.

Edwards caught a wild baby boar on the runway this morning. We were watching the snow falling when we noticed a huge boar strolling on the runway with four little ones behind. The moment he saw it, Edwards took off. We thought he was out of his mind. Surely the mother boar would turn on him and he'd be in big trouble. She didn't. She was running, and he was running, and the four sucklings were trying to keep up with the mother. We saw him dive and grab one. The mother didn't even look back.

Mace and I think we should eat him. Sgt. Briggs thinks it might not be a good idea. Like, it's French property and there's some kind of Army regulation about eating French property. In the meantime, the piglet—or what ever you call it—is very frightened. It won't eat anything we offer it, and Edwards wants to keep it as a pet. ·

There are no planes on the runway. None ever land. The runway is there in case of war. If the Russians cross the East German border, they'll be here in three days. Our woods are full of concealed trucks, jeeps, and armored vehicles, which three hundred or so soldiers keep in constant readiness. That is, they change the oil, check the pressure in the tires, and occasionally take them for a spin. The rest of the time they sit around dying of boredom, or they raise hell in Luneville or in their service club.

This "club," by the way, is just a shack with a few tables, chairs, and a jukebox. We don't go near the place unless we have to. We throw the drunks into our cells to sleep it off and in the morning send them back to their units.

We also have forty Poles under our jurisdiction. They pull guard duty around the post. They are what's left of the heroic General Anders's army, which fought alongside the Allies in the Italian campaign. These are people who couldn't emigrate or find some civilian employment. They are mostly in their fifties and they're all drunks. The Post Commander at times complains to Sgt. Briggs that he finds one of them asleep at the front gate, but no one does anything about it.

We had a debate this morning whether to give the piglet to the Poles or to our maintenance man, Francois. He was supposed to be coming to fix the toilet, and he's an enterprising, friendly sort of guy. We were still undecided when he showed up. The piglet was in the corner of the kitchen, looking sickly. It hadn't eaten anything in three days. "You want him?" Briggs said. Before the rest of us could react, Francois had the pig tied and thrown into his truck. Of course, we were invited to the roast. I knew none of us would go. We had looked too long into the eyes of that pig.

Tonight Briggs and I drove as far as St. Dié. It's a strange, modern-looking town, apparently completely rebuilt after being burnt down during the War. At the restaurant where we stopped to eat, they were surprised to see American soldiers. There are none in this area. They were friendly and the food was superb. After the second bottle of wine, it was hard to leave. Outside it was cold and snowing a little. "Not as bad as in South Dakota," Briggs said. He is a poor country boy. He loves the Army. He loves France, or more precisely, he loves a French waitress. He loves South Dakota too. As for me, I love wine and bean soup and sausages and good country bread.

On the way back we had a slight worry that there might be an emergency. For several miles the mountains prevented us from getting a clear radio reception, but the static told us something was going on. Suppose there was a serious car accident or a fight in a bar and they couldn't get in touch with us. There'd be hell to pay. It turned out to be just Mace asking for sandwiches and beer.

Today (Saturday) we had plenty to do for a change. At four in the afternoon we were playing cards, still not fully dressed, when the phone rang. There had been a knifing in the service club. Sgt. Briggs and I went in one jeep and Mace and Williams in the other. Edwards stayed by the radio. We got there so fast people were still running away from the club. Inside we almost stumbled on a man lying on the floor with a knife sticking out of his chest. Well, that took my breath away. Holy shit! This was serious business. The bartender pointed in the direction the culprits went. Briggs and I took out after them on foot while Mace called the medics.

Briggs was running ahead through the woods, and I was trying to keep after him, when we spotted a couple of guys ahead. One was running deeper into the woods, and the other was turning toward the open fields. Briggs yelled at me to take that one.

Here we were then, racing across the fields, with me out of breath calling on him to stop and falling behind, when I pulled out my pistol and fired once in the air. I didn't even think about it. I just wasn't going to run anymore. My man stopped instantly! He even fell on his knees with his back turned to me and waited for me to approach him. "I know my rights," he kept jabbering as I led him back to the club.

Briggs had gotten his pal. They were a couple of country boys whose life was made miserable by a mean sergeant. Today they could take it no more. By the time we brought them back to the station, they were in a party mood. They were laughing about it. "Did you see his face when that knife went in?" one of them kept saying to the other. Mace, a tough black dude from Detroit, was appalled by their hilarity. They were drunk, of course, and the man they stabbed wasn't dead. Still and all, that night Mace took me aside and warned me about rednecks. "They're all sick in the head," he said. He included Briggs and Edwards. He had a theory about it. "It's all that sheep fucking," he assured me.

I know something about that. One night in Toul, French cops came to our police station, and after much beating around the bush, finally blurted out that they had caught an American soldier fucking a farmer's sheep. When I got back to the barracks and reported to the card players what had happened, they all pretended astonishment at my astonishment. Didn't we fuck animals in the city?

Not many towns look good in the dead of winter, and Luneville is no exception. Its claim to fame is the once-elegant château where a certain Duchess Elizabeth-Charlotte fashioned a famous court that competed with Versailles in its splendor. Voltaire was supposed to be a frequent visitor. Perhaps he walked the gray streets of Luneville just as I'm doing now, imagining the life of Candide.

I find the place depressing. All this gray reminds me of prison. A town of family penitentiaries. Empty ones, perhaps? You walk its streets without meeting anyone. You enter a store, a dark one to be sure, and you wait forever before someone shuffles out from the back to serve you. In the bookstore, I'm the only customer. In the restaurant, too.

It gets better in the afternoon after the school lets out. There are even grown-ups to be seen shopping for food and having a drink. That goes on till about seven, when they all vanish. The streets are uncommonly dark, since all the houses have their shutters closed. Eight o'clock in the evening, and I'm the only one left, crossing a large square and wondering what happened to all the beautiful girls I saw earlier in the afternoon. Are they all undressed and in bed? Or are they gorging themselves in the dark at the family dinner table?

I say "in the dark" because I get the impression that these people don't want their neighbors to know what they're eating. They shop for *charcuteries* in the manner of spies picking up a roll of film at a secret drop. In the silence of wintry Luneville, I believe I hear them buttering their bread, slurping their evening soup, and cutting the meat they like underdone, almost bloody.

The weather is foul, of course. It's damp and raw and it snows a little. Then it sleets, making the roads treacherous. Last night we were returning from "Moon Town" when an MG with Army license plates passed us as at high speed on the curvy, tree-lined road. A drunk second lieutenant from our base, we figured.

A few miles ahead on the empty road we saw his tail lights at an odd angle. He had hit a tree head on. We heard his screams from inside the car, the front end of which was completely smashed. We tried to call the medics on the radio, but there was no contact. "Got to get on top of that hill," said Briggs and drove off leaving me with the screaming man.

Just then the last bus from Luneville came along full of

drunken soldiers. It stopped and the passengers stumbled out to take a look. The officer was still screaming, and the drunks wanted to pull him out of the wreck, but I wouldn't let them. We have to wait for the medics, that's the rule, I tried to explain.

Hell no! They were going to save the poor man right then and there and I could go fuck myself.

This was big trouble. A mean-looking crowd debating whether to lynch me or help that man. I was terrified and yet I couldn't let them do it. Again, I had to pull my gun out. Jesus Christ, they couldn't believe their eyes! A real bastard! Letting a man suffer like that.

They were just getting up the courage to charge me when Briggs and the medics showed up.

After much shouting back and forth, we sent the bus on its way and the two medics pulled the officer out of the wreck. When they got a better look at his bloody face, the one who seemed to be in charge passed out.

What a mess! There we were in the middle of the night on an empty road with a dying man and a passed out medic, and his sidekick was so frightened all he could do was wring his hands and shake his head.

Luckily for us, back at the base, Mace had had the sense to alert the French cops, who soon arrived with an ambulance from Luneville. We have only an infirmary on the base, so he had to be taken to a French hospital. That's what the cops did, and we followed them.

At the hospital they put the young officer on the table and somebody went to wake the doctor on duty. His legs looked badly broken, and his face had lacerations, but there were no other wounds anywhere on him. The only problem was, he was vomiting blood. "Internal injuries," said the sleepy young woman who was the doctor. They didn't want to open him here to see what was what and suggested we go to Nancy, at least twenty miles away. We decided to call the American hospital in Metz and ask them what to do. Of course, we got some idiot colonel on the line shouting that French hospitals stink, he wanted us to wait there till daybreak when he would send a helicopter. We asked the woman doctor her opinion. She shrugged her shoulders, and we understood we better get our fellow to Nancy *tout de suite.*

Off we went to Nancy, this time in a French ambulance. The roads were icy, but the driver was not holding back. "He's going to kill us all," I thought.

They were monitoring the officer's blood pressure, and it was falling dangerously. I could see it for myself. They had to give him several shots on the way. He moaned and we looked at each other without saying anything.

In Nancy at the big hospital, it was the same scene. They laid him on the emergency room table and stripped him naked. The elderly doctor who showed up didn't give us much confidence at first; he looked like an old drunk, unshaven, disheveled, and with a butt in the corner of his mouth. His hands, however, were beautiful. He passed them over the dying man's abdomen, touching him everywhere, almost caressing him. He was in no hurry and he kept puffing on his butt. Finally, he told us that there was no need to open him up. "He is going to be all right," he said. We were incredulous, worried the guy would die and we would end up being court-martialed for disobeying that colonel in Metz, but the doctor was adamant. Plus, his hands made us trust him. They were mesmerizing: the hands of a great musician or a thousand-dollar-a-night whore.

The officer is doing fine, we heard this afternoon. I'm still exhausted from lack of sleep and the excitment. I'm surprised how quickly we acted. We could have waited for that helicopter, although knowing how things work around here with Army, Air Force, and the French authorities, I doubt that it would have been there at daybreak. I have to hand it to Briggs. Most of the time he looks like a dopey hick, but last night he was lucidity itself. Him and that doc with his wise hands.

We were getting ready for the Poles' Christmas party. Briggs and I were in uniform since we were on duty, and Mace and Williams were in civvies. Edwards volunteered to stay by the radio since he doesn't drink. He loves Pepsi Cola, but you can get only Coke here. He's been miserable about that. His girlfriend in South Carolina sent him a gift package with two bottles of Pepsi. One of them fizzled out crossing the Atlantic, so he ended up with only one. He was going to drink it on Christmas Day, but this morning he discovered it was missing from his locker. Mace had hidden it. We watched Edwards search for it, even under his pillow and mattress. Finally, he came over to us, looking very pissed, and said: "Hey guys, where's my Pepsi?"

We told him he was nuts. We didn't know what the fuck he was talking about! And besides, we didn't give a shit about his Pepsi. Then we went back to what we were doing.

Poor Edwards sat on his bunk ready to cry. He sat and sat and wouldn't even have breakfast, he was so crushed. We had to slip out to the toilet to have a good laugh. In the end, when we gave him back the bottle, he made a little smile, but it vanished the moment Mace asked him if he'd give us all a sip on Christmas Day. Ha-ha-ha! We told him we were just kidding and he was happy again.

The Poles' Christmas party was outrageous. Being a Slav myself, I was seated next to the Captain, who kept feeding me choice morsels. They had all kinds of smoked fish, pâté, sausages, breads, pickled things, plus cases and cases of champagne and vodka. There were about thirty of us at the long table and everyone had a bottle of each in front of him and two large glasses, which had to be refilled after each toast. Standing on our feet, we toasted the many beauties of Poland and its women. We gulped the vodka and sipped the champagne. I was drunk after ten minutes, and so was everybody else. The pace was suicidal. The idea, obviously, was to go out of your mind as soon as possible. I've never seen anything like it. Briggs and I had to lower the flag in front of the headquarters at dusk, and dusk came right after lunch. We could hardly stand. As we were folding the flag in the prescribed military manner, we dropped it in the mud. Stars and stripes in the mud! Drunk on duty! They court-martial for less than that.

Luckily, no one saw us. We managed to pick it up and brush off the mud somehow. Then we went to bed. We never bothered to patrol that evening.

I went to spend three days in Strasbourg, but ended up in Paris. This is how it happened. I had the time off and thought, why not go see the famous cathedral and eat all that good Alsatian food! So I did. I took the train, arrived at Strasbourg in the early afternoon, found a hotel just across from the train station, and went to see the cathedral. It was magnificent. Still, if Gothic art is not your thing, and you hate the Church as an institution, the effect is purely aesthetic.

Then I walked the streets until time for dinner. The weather was dreary, with light snow falling and the women so bundled up you couldn't see what they looked like. I had an enormous meal of *choucroute* and a couple of bottles of the finest Riesling, and then I went to the movies and saw *Black Orpheus*. I had already seen it twice before in New York, but there was nothing else showing that looked interesting.

The movie ended a little before eleven, and I went straight to my hotel, undressed, jumped into bed, and turned off the lights. Just before I fell asleep, I suddenly asked myself: What in the world am I going to do in Strasbourg for two more days? Then I remembered that there was a train for Paris in ten minutes. All of a sudden I was wide awake. It took me five minutes to dress again, stun the night clerk by checking out in a hurry, and run across the empty square to the station.

There were not many people about. I bought a sleeping coach ticket, and by the time I reached the platform the train was pulling in with all its compartments darkened and its roofs covered with snow. Truly a midnight train. I was ushered to my compartment, where my bed was already made up. It was like a dream: half of me was still in that hotel bed snug under the down covers, and the other half was here undressing again. No one in the world knows where I am right now, it occurred to me. Not even my fate. I had walked out of my life like those people you read about in the papers who disappear without a trace after saying they're just going to the corner to buy a pack of cigarettes. I lay for hours in complete bliss. Why not take another train from Paris to Madrid? I had this enormous sense of freedom and well-being, and then I was sweetly tired, and the train seemed never to stop.

There's not much to do in Paris at six in the morning except sit in a chilly café, sipping coffee and reading the papers. Since it was much too early to call the friends with whom I usually stayed, I walked from Gare de L'Est to the Grand Boulevards. The morning was cold, so I had to keep a brisk pace. At some point, I began to crave bacon and eggs. I'd never seen anyone eat such food in a French café, but at the next one I asked the waiter if it were possible. He looked at me as though I were a lunatic. I ate four brioche just to appease him.

In the side streets off Boulevard Bonne Nouvelle, there were open bistros where workers were standing at the counter having a glass of red wine. After some hesitation, I went into one and ordered a glass with everybody watching. They could tell I was a foreigner, but were not sure what kind. I wasn't the type to be drinking red wine at seven in the morning. After a couple of glasses, I felt wonderful. Again there was this sense of freedom and adventure. I will do everything differently today, I swore to myself. I'll do things I never had the courage to do, like take a taxi to Rue St. Denis and pick up a whore. In the meantime, the sidewalks were getting busier. There were people to watch. I was having my third glass of red wine and had no intention of moving.

It's always the same. The last evening that I was in Paris there was a terrific party somewhere and the last train to Luneville left at 12:15. If I wasn't on that train and back at the post by

6:00 AM, I was officially AWOL. My outfit would cover for me for a while, but something might happen in my absence to bring officers from our headquarters in Toul.

So I spent the evening looking at my watch. The time seemed to fly. At eleven o'clock, I was talking to a beautiful girl who was interested in me. She had all the time in the world, while I was debating whether to miss the train. But I never do. I slipped out at the very last minute. I was the one running down the empty platform letting the conductor help me jump on the moving train.

This time I travelled second class, in a compartment full of snoring French soldiers who reeked of wine. I tried to sleep, too, but kept thinking about the party and the girl. I should have stayed, I thought. Once I did go AWOL to Paris—not because of a girl but because of a concert of black gospel music. That was when I was stationed in Toul. I went to pick up my pass on Saturday afternoon only to discover that it had been pulled. My bed wasn't made right during that morning's inspection, and I was being punished. I decided to go anyway. To hell with them. I had a reasonable expectation no one would be looking for me, and my buddies at the entrance gate would not be asking any questions. It was a terrific evening. But I was very worried when I returned on the midnight train, and did not sleep a wink. This trip I was awake with lovesickness and worried I would sleep through my stop.

As it turned out, I almost froze to death. I got off the local in St. Clement, having changed from the express in Luneville, and started walking to the base. It's about three or four miles up a hill, and the weather was bitter cold, the wind like a whip. I had only a raincoat on, with a sport jacket underneath but no sweater. On my feet I had a pair of light Italian shoes. After a while, my feet started to go numb. It was like walking on air. "Walk faster," I told myself. The higher I got the more cutting the wind was. I could feel each rib, each bone in my body. And then I couldn't. One part of me wanted to sit down and rest and the other realized the danger. Then I saw the gates of our post and the Polish guard, who had walked out to see who was coming on foot so early. What he saw made him run back into the guardhouse for his thermos. Wise Pole, he had vodka in it. I took a big gulp, and then another right there on the road. He led me by the hand into his warm shack, where I continued drinking. The old man was delighted to be of service and kept urging me to drink more. I didn't even get drunk. Finally I walked the rest of the way, found everyone asleep in our station, and went to bed myself.

We were summoned to the main barracks this afternoon, which was strange. They hardly ever call us, even at night when everyone's drunk and getting into fights. They break them up themselves, and that's just fine with us. I've seen MP's in Toul get badly beaten in such situations. You have to have a lot of experience and luck to get out unharmed. "Act quickly," an old sergeant once told me. "Pluck the offender and beat it. Don't stand around arguing military regulations with the drunks."

But this was different. When Mace and Edwards arrived, only a couple of sergeants and an officer were waiting, looking embarrassed. They brought out a short, shy-looking black guy and asked that he be taken into custody. It seems—and this took a while to get straight—he was caught sucking the dick of a corporal who was taking a nap after lunch. A fishy story. Like, supposedly, the corporal's dick had fallen out of his underwear, and he never woke up while the accused was giving him a blow job. They wanted the man out of there while they made arrangements to ship him back to his unit in Germany. Afraid of a lynch mob and the rest.

Mace told us all this while we sat in our station drinking coffee and studying the accused, who stood before us looking miserable.

"Is that true, Willie?" Briggs hollered at him, but poor Willie just hung his head and said nothing.

Willie has been with us four days, and we are used to him. Last night, when Briggs and I came back from patrol, he was playing poker with Mace, Williams, and Edwards.

"The cocksucker's taking all our money," Williams told us, and even Willie had to smile.

Williams wants to take Willie to a whorehouse and straighten him out. He makes him sit for hours at the desk and go through his collection of Scandinavian girlie magazines in preparation. From time to time, he checks on him: "How do you like that, Willie?" he says, pointing to some hairy crotch while studying the reaction in Willie's eyes.

Willie is a scrawny, sensitive looking New York boy. He has a flute, which he plays beautifully when we leave him alone. "Is that Bach?" I asked him one time, and he nodded gravely.

Briggs makes him work. He sweeps, washes the dishes, scrubs the bathroom. Our place never looked better. We are going to miss him when they take him away.

We keep telling Willie he'll get a medical discharge, but that doesn't seem to cheer him up. It's his father he's worried about, he told me. He also confessed that he thought we were going to beat him when he first came. I explained that we never beat anybody up because there's too much paperwork afterwards if you leave marks. The other guys still call him a cocksucker, but I get the impression that he likes it here and wouldn't mind staying with us. "Even the cocksucker knows we got it made," Williams announces, and we all nod in agreement.

They took poor Willie away. That night it was snowing like hell and the roads were in bad shape. Mace and I patrolled Luneville, but there were no GI's in town. We made the usual tour of the seedy bars, where all the whores were accounted for. It would have been a perfect night for listening to French torch songs on the old record player, but the juke boxes were reserved for American pop and their French imitators. With no customers to worry about, the owners offered us drinks, and we accepted. Good cognac, not the rotgut they sell to the dumb sailors. In one joint the Madame even offered us girls, in the spirit of the holiday season, but we refused. Her whores looked like they must've been hustling when General Patton passed through in 1944. They thought us refusing like that was very funny, and they made sucking noises with their lips, lifting their skirts to their crotches. They think the world of us since we broke up a bloody fight for them a couple of weeks ago. They know they can call us if some soldier gets nasty. We come and take him off by the scruff of his neck.

The snow was still coming down hard; even our jeep was slipping and sliding. We made one more stop, at the Café de la Gare. There was no one there except the boss and a couple of cab drivers waiting for the Paris train, which was late. Here, too, everyone was glad to see us. Drinks on the house—because of Mace, I thought to myself. The French have a thing about American blacks, especially when they're as tall and good looking as Mace. Their own blacks they think are shit, but for Mace their eyes were full of admiration.

They wanted to know if we have such crummy weather where we come from. You bet, we told them. Ten times worse. That made them happy. Then the conversation turned to the subject of GI's, the way they behave in public places. They cause problems, we agreed; some of them are morons. They were glad to hear us say that. We made faces and they made faces to emphasize the point. No doubt about it. The world is full of people like that.

In the seven months I've been in Toul and Luneville, I haven't met any girls. I talk to cops, whores, café owners, waiters, and the like, but that's as far as it goes. It is impossible to meet girls my age. Occasionally I come across one and attempt to start a conversation. They reply briefly, politely, and suspiciously, and I get the impression they've been warned: If I catch you talking to an American, I'll kill you. Who can blame them?

Once in Nancy a family showed up at our downtown MP station—father, mother, and teenage daughter with a siz-able belly—wanting to know about a certain corporal. We made a few calls and found out that the fellow had been discharged and was living somewhere in Oregon. All three of them hung their heads and stood there a long time, not knowing what to say or do next. They didn't have the vaguest idea where Oregon was. Finally they shuffled out without another peep.

We have a new post commander. He barged into our quarters without a warning while we were still lazing in bed. It was almost noon. His eyes popped out when he saw the mess. Since my bunk is closest to the door, he started chewing me out first. Are you some kind of prima donna, he kept screeching over and over, as he poked with his foot at the dirty clothes on the floor. I never hung up any of my things, and nobody else did either. In my locker, where regulations specified my headgear should be, I kept bottles of wine. The other guys had beer. The upshot was, he would come back in three hours and the place would be so clean he could eat off the floor, or we would be in big trouble.

Well, we didn't bust our balls. We stuffed most of our things in laundry bags and stashed them in our jeeps outside. When he returned, there were only a few items, properly displayed, to look at in our lockers. You could see he was puzzled, but couldn't think of anything to say just then. Besides, there was the business of law and order to discuss. We exaggerated our problems—the continual knifings, so many fags running around, and so on. By now we were sitting in the station, beginning to relax a little around the elderly colonel. All of a sudden, he let out a shriek! We thought the Russians were at the door and looked in the direction he was pointing, but there was nothing to see. Just Private Williams drinking water from a faucet.

"He is drinking French water!" the colonel screamed.

So what? We drink French water all the time, and it tastes really good. Would he like to try a glass?

He couldn't believe his ears! The whole United States Army could be incapacitated! What irresponsibility! The Commies would finally make that surprise attack starting the Third

World War, and the American Army would be in the latrine having the shits! He was going to put a stop to it right there and then.

He got on the phone, announced a national emergency, and ordered someone to bring us American water. They were to deliver a whole tanker of the best American water and leave it in the garage exclusively for our use. Anytime we were thirsty, we could just go out there and turn on the spigot. That way we would be safe, the Army would be safe, and the Western democracies would be safe.

When he left we looked at each other in disbelief. You meet a lot of dummies among the officers, but this fellow topped them all. You watch, said Mace, this is not the end of it. There are plenty of other crazy notions where that one came from.

The tank of American water arrived. We all drank a glass just to see if there was any difference. There was none that we could tell. It was probably French water someone was passing off as American. There had to be a scam—but better that than the thought that they had ships crossing the Atlantic full of Jersey water.

The Poles came to ask us our opinion of the new colonel. He's a raving lunatic, we told them. They were delighted. It seems he complained to their commander that the guards' shoes were not spit shined. These were fifty-year-old, overweight alcoholics whom Stalin had sent to Siberia in 1939 and whom General Andrews had rescued and led, via Persia and Egypt, into the battle for Italy in 1944; now an American colonel wanted them to spend their evenings spitting on shoes and polishing belt buckles!

And besides, outside it was sleeting and muddy.

I purchased an anthology of poetry, *Le Livre d'Or de la Poesie Française,* in a Luneville bookstore. The old sourpuss who owns the joint was surprised to see an MP buying a book like that. She gave me a searching look while handing me my change, suspicious and mystified. That pleased me immensely. I gave my best imitation of nonchalance as I walked slowly out and climbed into the jeep.

Cendrars was my man then. Described in the anthology as the "grand voyager," Cendrars abandoned his studies at the age of sixteen "pour courir le monde." I love his "Easter in New York" and his "Transsiberian Prose," which were included:

> En ce temps-là j'étais en mon adolescence.
> J'avais à peine seize ans et je me souvenais déjà plus de mon enfance.
> J'étais à seize mille lieues du lieu de ma naissance.

If you don't watch it, Simic, I told myself, you're going to regress from being a super modernist to a full-blooded Romantic!

True. A certain kind of sentimentality got to me. I had a great weakness, for instance, for the French popular singers of before the war: Frehel, Piaf, Lucienne Delyle, Lucienne Boyer. They made me wallow in self-pity, made me want to go AWOL and spend the rest of my life hiding in some Marseille dive, with a cigarette in the corner of my mouth, listening to a blind guy play the accordion. I could think of a dozen possible lives, each more heartbreaking than the other. While I listened to these songs, I wanted to be the bartender of that dive, in love with a street-walker who was a cocaine addict, but had a heart of gold.

In the meantime, my buddies told me I had a terrific future in police work. The New York Police Department would welcome me with open arms, thanks to my training and extensive experience. I would live like a king, taking bribes left and right, then retire to Florida after twenty years. They didn't realize I saw myself as a fall guy in one of these French songs I was listening to. I would spend the rest of my life in some seedy hotel off Place Blanche, reaching under the bed for a bottle of cheap red.

The French cops called us to say that a soldier had climbed the train station roof and was trying to adjust the big hand of the clock. We went to see. They had to bring a fire truck with ladders to haul him down. He was still very drunk, but we asked him anyway why he had done it. The clock was five minutes fast, he told us.

Another call from the French, this time from the gendarmes who are the Federal Police: A longtime American deserter from a unit in Germany was apparently holed up in a hotel room in Épinal. We checked our files, found his name, and discovered that he was also believed to be extremely dangerous. That's what we told the gendarmes when we went to see them. They seemed delighted by the news. "Boom, boom," they shouted, winking and grinning at us. The plan was to arrive at the hotel at the crack of dawn when the deserter was in a deep sleep and break into his room with guns drawn.

We got to Épinal late, had a long supper with the gendarmes, and then went to their local station to wait for the morning. A long night of Sgt. Briggs's army and police stories, to which the French reciprocated with their own, all of which I had to translate.

There were two of us and four of them. It was past four o'clock. The French were loading their guns. That made me wide awake. I could imagine a gun fight and a stray bullet hitting me. The thought of firing myself worried me too. What if I killed someone? Every other time I had pulled the pistol in the past, it was to fire into the air. Then I had that option; this was different.

At the hotel, the owner and his wife were waiting for us. They'd been warned. The deserter was asleep in a room on the second floor. We took our boots off, cocked our guns, and went up, one creaky stair after the other, the terrified owner right after us. On the second floor we came to a stop. Absolute silence. Winter. Snow outside.

We moved again, taking a long time to reach the door of room seventeen. One of the gendarmes was going to kick it in, and we were all going to rush in with guns pointed. The bed, we were told, was in the middle of the room facing the door.

Jesus! The noise as they broke in, with me lagging behind! In an instant the man in bed had five guns pressed against his head. I thought his eyes would jump out of their sockets. We were all frozen like that for a minute or two, and then Briggs grabbed him by the hair, dragged him out of bed, threw him against the wall, kicked his legs apart, and started to search him. This seemed pointless to me; the poor guy had only a T-shirt and underwear on. No place to hide a weapon. Plus, he looked harmless. A tall, skinny fellow who may have been dying of starvation. The French, however, loved Briggs's rough stuff. "Comme chez nous," they squealed happily while nudging each other.

Well, it turned out the tough guy didn't even own a nail file. Nothing dangerous about him. He was a cook in some outfit in Germany. A religious nut. Perhaps a little feebleminded. They all made fun of him. On the way to Nancy he told us about talking to God only last night. Briggs thought it was all an act. I didn't know what to think. He couldn't have been that innocent if he got as far as Épinal.

"Fuck them all!" Briggs says, and we all nod in agreement. We have no way to figure out why people act the way they do; we are not psychiatrists or father confessors. Our idea of happiness is NOTHING HAPPENS. What others would consider total boredom, we consider bliss. We get it, too. Three days go by without a single call. Everybody is behaving because the weather stinks. Let it stay like this forever. I've got my books, I've got my radio and my wine.

In two weeks I'm returning to my unit in Toul. I'll never be able to readjust to the regular army routine. Just to make my life miserable, the bastards there will make me direct traffic at the main gate the first day I get back. I'll wear white gloves and be expected to salute every officer in his car and be in every respect a model of military bearing and neatness.

I remember once being so hungover I didn't see the general—actually I did see him, but too late—and didn't salute. He got out of his car and dressed me down while the traffic stood still and everyone sat in their vehicles enjoying themselves. The sergeant on duty screamed at me for half an hour when he found out what happened. The company commander yelled at me in front of the whole company the next day.

"Fuck them all," says Briggs again and we all concur.

Briggs is going to marry his waitress, a big, strong widow with a couple of small kids. Not bad looking, but all the same, what is she going to do on a farm in South Dakota? They don't have a language in common. Briggs still hasn't learned more than two words of French, and her English is not much better.

On the other hand, the village she lives in is a dump. Only Mace loves the countryside around here: he wants to stay in Europe after he is discharged, travel, work, come back to France, eventually buy a small café with his savings.

"I'll spend the rest of my life visiting you guys," I tell them. I'll go see Williams and his whorehouse in LA, check out Briggs on his farm, visit Edwards in his shit-hole in South Carolina, and Mace himself will serve me Pernod when I drop by his café in St. Clement. They all love the idea, and we spend the rest of the evening imagining these visits, knowing all along that we'll never see each other again after we part company here.

Edwards never goes anywhere on his own. He doesn't understand why we do. "What's in Paris?" he wants to know. We tell him about the beauty of the city, the good-looking streetwalkers in furs, the night clubs with nude dancing. "Nothing!" A waste of money, as far as he is concerned.

He's never been anywhere in the States either. We want to take him to a high-class restaurant in Luneville for a farewell dinner, but he's suspicious of French cooking. "It's better than the shit you eat at home," Mace tells him. He doesn't believe that for a moment. The Frenchies he sees on the base are not much to look at, poor farm folk from surrounding villages. Dressed half in their rags, half in our army clothes, they look like bums. When they grin, they usually have a couple of teeth missing. As for their patois, even I don't have a clue. Of course, they take home everything they can slip past the Poles at the gate, but who cares? From time to time we do a surprise stop and search, make them strip, collect piles of army clothes, equipment, tools, wire, spoons, forks, everything but a tank! They stand there trembling in the cold, thinking they will lose their jobs, swearing by everything that's holy that they have no idea how the stuff got into their pockets. We tell them to forget it! No sweat. Uncle Sam is generous. Nothing to worry about. They can't believe their ears. Mouths hanging open in disbelief. Then an eruption! Joy! They want to hug and kiss us, take us home for a meal.

Anyway, these are the only French Edwards knows, and it takes us all day to convince him that he must come along and eat with us in Luneville. "It's an order," Briggs barks out finally because Edwards keeps whining and changing his mind.

"Doesn't want to be seen with a nigger in a public place," is Mace's opinion. Could be.

Whatever the case, we drag the Carolina hick to the best restaurant in town, where we proceed to order a large, elegant meal. With Edwards, of course, we are extremely cautious: just steak and fries for the redneck. First, however, he has to try some smoked salmon. Again, a direct military order from his superior.

Edwards takes a teeny morsel, chews on it forever, then finally allows himself a little smile. He likes it! An order of your best smoked salmon just for private Edwards, we yell to the waitress. Later he even confesses that he likes the fries. The best fries he ever had in his life! And the steak is good, too.

Now comes the hardest part. We have to make him take a sip of red wine. He won't hear of it. It's against his religious beliefs. "He thinks they were drinking Pepsi at the Last Supper," Mace says.

I have an idea, however. I notice Edwards is eyeing the pretty waitress, who keeps looking at him, too. I'm going to ask her to ask him to try the wine. That's what I do, in French so he doesn't understand. She goes over to him, pours the wine into his glass, and with the sexiest smile tells him that this wine is "very special," and would he please try it as a favor to her. Edwards sits there blushing, thinking it over forever. Then, all of a sudden, he picks up the glass with all of us breathlessly watching, and takes a cautious sip. It's a miracle! We all applaud. "It's good," he says and takes a bigger sip. We are so happy we are kissing each other drunkenly. It's because we are not too far from Jeanne d'Arc's birthplace, I explain. The region is predisposed toward miracles, as you can see.

Red Knight

When my father's father, who came from a line of village blacksmiths, wanted to upset my mother, who was a member of an old and distinguished Belgrade family, he would take some well-known Serbian heroic ballad and turn it around. So, instead of Prince Marko going out early one morning to fight Turks, he would lose his drawers and spend the rest of the day looking for them. These improvised parodies appalled my mother and delighted my grandfather and father. I was caught in between. I tried my best to keep a straight face.

The songs in this collection echo the heroic ballads and the short lyrics in that tradition. They employ familiar narrative strategies and literary conceits for similarly subversive ends. My mother, who was not a prude, found such irreverence shocking. "Some things are sacred," she'd say, and who could argue with that? The traditional ballads and songs are works of great delicacy of feeling. They are the pride of the Serbian people. How could one possibly make fun of them?

Middle-class city dwellers, like my mother, are always surprised by the realities of folk life and culture. I remember a Paris-educated cousin of ours claiming once that Serbian peasants never use bad language. His reasoning went like this: the country folk must be angelically pure, since they are the moral foundation of our people.

Even at the age of ten I knew better, since I spent summers in my grandfather's village playing with the children my cousin romanticized.

Introduction to *Red Knight,* an anthology of Serbian women's folk songs.

> Sonny-boy, Milutine,
> What's that hanging down your thighs?

the little girls sang as I walked by, turning red in the face. Sober minds, tender souls, schoolteachers, policemen, priests would all shout in a chorus that this is in no way representative of the Serbian people! They are the very ones, of course, who prohibited the publication of this collection for almost two hundred years.

It's the revenge of the yokels, this collection is. The peasant storytellers—and this is true in all cultures—do not just tell their tales and sing their songs to be amusing. There's an undercurrent of realism, of spite, especially in comic pieces. Tragedy is a cosmic matter; comedy concerns individual lives in their dailiness. These poems tell us more about how Serbian peasants actually lived than many of the heroic and lyric songs.

For instance, to give a single example, till very recently in rural households everybody slept in one bed. I saw it with my own eyes when I was a child. Grown-ups and children and even guests climbed into the same huge bed. What went on under the heavy covers anyone can imagine. There were no mysteries about sex, even for the smallest child.

That everything comes down to the body is the wisdom of the comic and the erotic. You can talk all you want about heroes and saints and the rest, but in the end it's the belly and the reproductive organs that matter. Truth is naked and laughing. Women, as these songs prove, always knew that better than men.

The tradition is old, of course. The ribaldry of medieval carnivals and feasts and trickster tales everywhere is part of it. We find it also in early American blues:

> Your nuts hang down like a damn church clapper,
> And your dick stands up like a steeple,

sings one Lucille Bogan.

The joys of good sex and the failure of men to perform adequately are the subject of both. "Fucking is a thing that will take me to heaven," says Bogan. There are many Serbian counterparts to this.

> I thought, Mama,
> I was going to fly.

Sex is exhilarating and hilarious. Come to think of it, there's nothing funnier than sex, if you ask these folk.

There are darker overtones, too, in these songs. Incest and especially rape are frequent. Beware of priests and monks especially, the songs are saying. All these pious hypocrites, mumblers of Holy Masses and snatchers of poor people's coins, are dangerous. We are in a world of drunkards, gluttons, and horny devils masquerading as Christians. The laughter, at times, is ambivalent, derisive, and terrified.

Still, merriment prevails. Mainly, these are songs in praise of the erotic. They delight in the body and its appetites and rejoice in our human foolishness. They bring us good cheer the world's horrors and deceits could not silence.

The Minotaur Loves His Labyrinth

The ideal place to teach creative writing is a used book store, says my friend Vava Hristić.

I'm writing for a school of philosophers who will feast, who will be remembered for asking for a third and fourth helping of the same dish while discussing metaphysics. Philosophers who seek those moments in which the senses, the mind, and the emotions are experienced together.

My hunch that language is inadequate when speaking about experience is really a religious idea, what they call negative theology.

The ambition of much of today's literary theory seems to be to find ways to read literature without imagination.

What all reformers and builders of utopias share is the fear of the comic. They are right. Laughter undermines discipline and leads to anarchy. Humor is anti-utopian. There was more truth in jokes Soviets told than in all the books written on the USSR.

My old poems on Geometry (The Point, Triangle, Euclid Avenue, The Ballad of the Wheel) are my attempt to read between Euclid's lines.

New York City is much too complex a place for just one god and one devil.

From "Notebooks 1987–1993."

The most original achievement of American literature is the absence of an official literary language.

Where time and eternity intersect my consciousness is the traffic cop holding up a STOP sign.

Ethics of reading. Does the critic have any moral responsibility toward the author's intentions? Of course not, say all the hip critics. What about the translator? Isn't the critic, too, a translator? Would we accept a translation of Dante's *Divine Comedy* which would disregard the poet's intentions?

Gombrowicz, too, used to wonder, how is it that good students understand novels and poems, while literary critics mostly talk nonsense.

The ambition of literary realism is to plagiarize God's creation.

Seeing is determined not by the eye but by the clarity of my consciousness. Most of the time the eyes see nothing.

In their effort to divorce language and experience, deconstructionist critics remind me of middle-class parents who do not allow their children to play in the street.

Lately in the United States we have been caught between critics who do not believe in literature and writers who believe only in naive realism. Imagination continues to be what everybody pretends does not exist.

Many of our critics read literature like totalitarian cops on the lookout for subversive material—for instance, the claim that there is a world outside language.

Poetry tries to bridge the abyss lying between the name and the thing. That language is a problem is no news to poets.

Poets worth reading usually believe things the age they live in no longer does. Poets are always anachronistic, obsolete, unfashionable, and permanently contemporary.

Can a timeless moment of consciousness ever be adequately conveyed in a medium that depends on time, i.e., language? This is the mystic's and the lyric poet's problem.

A good-tasting homemade stew of angel and beast.

One point of agreement between Eastern and Western philosophy: men live like fools.

Wisdom as measure, as a sense of proportion, as middle ground. If it's defined that way, one sees why there are only a few examples of wisdom in the entire history of the world.

If Derrida is right, all that the poets have ever done is whistle in the dark.

Like many others, I grew up in an age that preached liberty and built slave camps. Consequently, reformers of all varieties terrify me. I only need to be told that I'm being served a new, improved, low-fat baked ham, and I gag.

It's the desire for irreverence as much as anything else that brought me first to poetry. The need to make fun of authority, break taboos, celebrate the body and its functions, claim that one has seen angels in the same breath as one says that there is no god. Just thinking about the possibility of saying shit to everything made me roll on the floor with happiness.

Here's Octavio Paz at his best: "The poem will continue to be one of the few resources by which man can go beyond himself to find out what he is profoundly and originally."

The sense of myself existing comes first. Then come images and then language.

Being is not an idea in philosophy, but a wordless experience we have from time to time.

Suppose you don't believe in either Hobbes's notion that man is evil and society is good, or Rousseau's that man is good and society evil. Suppose you believe in the hopeless and messy mixture of everything.

I know a fellow who reads modern poetry only in the john.

Here's a quick recipe on how to make a modern poem out of an old one. Just take out the beginning and the end; the invocation to the Muses and the nicely wrapped up final message.

I still think Camus was right. Heroic lucidity in the face of the absurd is about all we really have.

Fourier, who planned a model of perfect human society, was known never to laugh. There you have it! Collective happiness under the steely gaze of a murderer.

A true confession: I believe in a soluble fish.

A school where the best students are always kicked out, there you have the history of the academy's relationship to contemporary art and literature. (I think Valery said something like that.)

The prose poem is the result of two contradictory impulses, prose and poetry, and therefore cannot exist, but it does. This is the sole instance we have of squaring the circle.

First you simplify whatever is complex, you reduce reality to a single concept, and then you start a church of some kind. What surprises me endlessly is how every new absolutism, every one-sided worldview is instantly attractive to so many seemingly intelligent people.

My soul is constituted of thousands of images I cannot erase. Everything I remember vividly, from a fly on the wall in Belgrade to some street in San Francisco early one morning. I'm a grainy old, often silent, often flickering film.

Only poetry can measure the distance between ourselves and the Other.

Form in a poem is like the order of performing acts in a circus.

One writes because one has been touched by the yearning for and the despair of ever touching the Other.

We call "street wise" someone who knows how to look, listen, and interpret the teeming life around him. To walk down a busy city block is a critical act. Literature, aesthetics, and psychology all come into play.

Nationalists and religious fundamentalists all hate the modern city because of its variety and spontaneity. Stupidity and ill will easily rule in a small community, but in a city one has many ways of eluding its grasp.

Hopscotch. Pierre leapt from Stalin to Mao to Pol Pot to Saddam. I hope after the experience of this century that no one in the future will still believe the myth of the critical independence of the intellectuals.

The lyric poem is often a scandalous assertion that the private is public, that the local is universal, that the ephemeral is eternal. And it happens! The poets turn out to be right. This is what the philosophers cannot forgive the poets.

How many literary theorists and teachers of literature truly understand that poems are not written merely for the sake of oneself, or for the sake of some idea, or for the sake of the reader, but out of a deep reverence for the old and noble art of poetry.

We speak of rhyme as a memory aid, but not of striking images and unusual similitudes that have a way of making themselves impossible to forget.

I love Mina Loy's "No man whose sex life was satisfactory ever became a moral censor."

Since democracy does not believe in the exclusive possession of truth by one party, it is incompatible with nationalism and religion, I tell my Yugoslav friends.

My aspiration is to create a kind of nongenre made up of fiction, autobiography, the essay, poetry, and of course, the joke!

A theory of the universe: the whole is mute; the part screams with pain or guffaws.

I would like to write a book that would be a meditation on all kinds of windows. Store windows, monastic windows, windows struck by sunlight on a street of dark windows, windows in which clouds are reflected, imaginary windows, hotel windows, prisons . . . windows one peeks out of or peeks in. Windows that have the quality of religious art, etc.

Rushdie's case proves that literature is the dangerous activity, not literary criticism and its currently fashionable notion that literature is merely the propaganda of the ruling ideology.

Here's the totalitarian theory of literature from Plato to the Inquisition to Stalin and all their followers:

1. Separation of content and form, ideas from experience. Literature is primarily its content.
2. The content needs to be unmasked, revealed for what it truly is. The cop slapping the young poet and demanding to know who ordered him to write like that is the secret ideal.
3. Literature is clever propaganda for a particular cause.

4. Literature on its own terms is socially dangerous. Pure art is a blasphemy against authority.
5. The poet and the writer are never to be trusted. Trust the critic and the censor for their constant vigilance.

What is the difference between a reader and a critic? The reader identifies with the work of literature, the critic keeps a distance in order to see the shape it makes. The reader is after pleasure, the critic wants to understand how it works. The erotic and the hermeneutic are often at odds and yet they should be companions.

A New Hampshire high school student reading an ancient Chinese poem and being moved—a theory of literature that cannot account for that commonplace miracle is worthless.

Another large group of cultural illiterates we are stuck with: college professors who do not read contemporary literature or know modern art, modern music, theater, cinema, jazz, etc.

Eternity is the insomnia of Time. Did somebody say that, or is it my idea?

If poems were the expression of one's ethnicity they would remain local, but they are written by individuals in all cultures, which makes them universal.

Both imagination and the experience of consciousness affirm that each is all and all is each. Metaphors (seeing resemblance everywhere) are internationalist in spirit. If I were a nationalist, I'd prohibit the use of a metaphor.

For Emily Dickinson every philosophical idea was a potential lover. Metaphysics is the realm of eternal seduction of the spirit by ideas.

The individual is the measurer, the world is what is measured, and the language of poetry is the measure. There! Now you can hang me by my tongue!

How do we know the Other? By being madly in love.

Comes a time when the living moment expands. The instant becomes roomy. It opens up. Suddenly everything inside and outside of ourselves is utterly different. I know what I am, and I know what I am not. It's just me and It.

Is the clarity of consciousness the negation of imagination? One can imagine plenty in a state of semiconsciousness.

The highest levels of consciousness are wordless and its lowest gabby.

The tribe always wants you to write about "great and noble subjects."

When I was little, bad boys in my neighborhood advised me to grab my balls every time I saw a priest. It's the first lesson in the arts I was given.

Seeing the familiar with new eyes, that quintessential idea of modern art and literature, the exile and the immigrant experience daily.

Here's Konstantin Nojka's observation, with which I agree completely: "Thought precedes the word—as in the example of a little kid who calls a strange man 'dad.' The adults correct him and say it's not daddy, but what the kid means is that he's like dad—has the same height, glasses, etc."

The academics always believe that they have read more than the poets, but this has rarely been my experience. Poets of my generation and the preceding generation are far better read than their academic contemporaries, with exceptions, of course, on both sides.

Christ, like Sappho, challenges the tribe. Their message is, you have no tribal obligations, only love for the Father in the first case and love of your own solitude in the second.

Consciousness: this dying match that sees and knows the name of what it throws its brief light upon.

Imagination equals Eros. I want to experience what it's like to be inside someone else in the moment when that someone is being touched by me.

I'm in the business of translating what cannot be translated: being and its silence.

Ars Poetica: trying to make your jailers laugh.

Two young birch trees wrestling in the wind. The crow in the snow refereeing.

Here where they make piggy banks with the face of Jesus.

Strafford, New Hampshire, Orpheus assuaging the fierceness of wild beasts with his new kazoo.

The day I went to make funeral arrangements for my father-in-law, I caught a glimpse of the mortician's wife nursing the mortician's new daughter. Her breasts were swollen huge with milk.

A sequel to Dante's *Divine Comedy:* the modern hero retraces his steps from heaven to hell.

I have a House of Horrors the size of my head, or the size of the known universe. It doesn't matter which.

Like everybody else, I'm betting everything on the remote possibility that one of many lies will come true. I say to myself in moments of tenderness, perhaps you're more of a philosopher than you know.

As for the ALWAYS OPEN, always brightly lit House of Horrors, it's just a windowless room, empty except for some trash on the floor.

The Gestapo and the KGB were also convinced that the personal is political. Virtue by decree was their other belief.

The closeness of two people listening together to music they both love. There's no more perfect union. I remember a summer evening, a good bottle of white wine, and Helen and I listening to Prez play "Blue Lester." We were so attentive, as only those who have heard a piece a hundred times can be, so this time it seemed the piece lasted forever.

The lost thread of a dream. What a pretty phrase!

She's a passionate believer in multiculturalism, but she objects to all that fatty ethnic food. Especially sausages! No good for you.

Cioran is right when he says that "we are all religious spirits without a religion."

Eurocentricism is the dumbest idea ever proposed by academics. The notion that all European history—all its philosophy, literature, art, cuisine, martyrdom, oppression—is the expression of a single ideology belongs in the *National Enquirer* on the same page with "I was Bigfoot's Loveslave."

Even as I concentrate all my attention on the fly on the table, I glance fleetingly at myself.

America is the only country in the world where a rich woman with servants can speak of being a woman oppressed and not be laughed at.

What the lyric poets want is to convert their fragment of time into eternity. It's like going to the bank and expecting to get a million dollars for your nickel.

I agree with Isaiah Berlin when he says in an interview: "I do not find all-embracing systems congenial." I have a horror of minds who see all events as instances of universal rules and principles. I believe in the deep-set messiness of everything. I associate tidiness with dictatorship.

How to kill the innate poetry of children—the secret agenda of a conference on primary school education. I met teachers who fear poetry the way vampires fear the cross.

For a man like Teller, science meant new and much improved ways of killing people, and he was enthusiastically received in high places.

It is in the works of art and literature that one has the richest experience of the Other. When the experience is truly powerful, we can be anybody, a nineteenth-century Russian prince, a fifteenth-century Italian harlot.

Most of our political writers on the left and the right are interchangeable. That's why it was child's play for so many liberals to become neoconservatives. What serenity the day one realizes that!

Here's one firm law of history: truth is known at precisely that point in time when nobody gives a shit.

A poem is an invitation to a voyage. As in life, we travel to see fresh sights.

To be an exception to the rule is my sole ambition.

Twenty years ago the poem for me was still mostly an inspired and unpremeditated utterance. My friend Vasko Popa on the other hand, was all calculation. A poem was an act of supreme critical intelligence for him. He had already thought out everything he was going to write for the rest of his life. Once late at night, after much wine, he described to me in detail his future poems. He wasn't putting me on. In later years I'd see these poems come into print one by one, and they were just as he described them that night.

Popa's metaphysics was Symbolist, and yet it's not so much that he used symbols in his poetry, and he did. What he really wanted to understand is the secret of how symbols are made.

Poetry is sacred action, it's been said. Popa's poems demonstrate how the laws of the imagination work.

"The salad bird" writes Lucian, "is an enormous bird covered all over with salad greens instead of feathers; its wings look exactly like lettuce leaves." For Popa, language was not an abstract system but a living idiom, an idiom already full of poetic invention. In that respect, his imagination and his poetry are wholly determined by the language in which he wrote. In his poems the reader enters the Serbian language and meets the gods and demons hiding there.

Little said, much meant, is what poetry is all about. An idiom is the lair of the tribal beast. It carries its familiar smell. We are here in the realm of the submerged and elusive meanings that do not correspond to any actual word on the page. Lyricism, in its truest sense, is the awe before the untranslatable. Like childhood, it is a language that cannot be replaced by any other language. A great lyric poem must approach untranslatability.

Translation is an actor's medium. If I cannot make myself believe that I'm writing the poem I'm translating, no degree of aesthetic admiration for the work can help me.

The philosophical clear-sightedness of a man who is taking a long siesta on a day when many important matters should be attended to. As somebody said, cats know laziness is divine.

Blues musicians do not doubt that music touches the soul.

My poem "Midpoint" is a reduction, the cutting down to a kind of algebraic equation of a ten-page poem on cities where I have lived. The paring down occurred when I realized that all my future cities are the ghost images of the city where I was born. In my imagination I'm always at midpoint.

To be bilingual is to realize that the name and the thing are not bound intrinsically. It is possible to find oneself in a dark hole between languages. I experience this now when I speak

Serbian, which I no longer speak fluently. I go expecting to find a word, knowing that there was a word there once, and find instead a hole and a silence.

I grew up among some very witty people, I now realize. They knew how to tell stories and how to laugh and that has made all the difference.

The restaurant is Greek. The waiter's name is Socrates, so Plato must be in the kitchen, and Aristotle is the fellow studying a racing form at the cash register.

Today's special: grilled calamari with fresh parsley, garlic, and olive oil.

When I started writing poetry in 1955 all the girls I wanted to show my poems to were American. I was stuck. It was never possible for me to write in my native language.

I prefer Aristophanes to Sophocles, Rabelais to Dante. There's as much truth in laughter as there is in tragedy, a view not shared by many people. They still think of comedy as nose-thumbing at the serious things in life.

My second-grade teacher in Belgrade told me more than forty-five years ago that I was a "champion liar." I still remember being mortally offended and kind of flattered.

Only through poetry can human solitude be heard in the history of humanity. In that respect, all the poets who ever wrote are contemporaries.

A scene from French movies of the fifties that I still love: A fly gets shut in a room with three armed thugs and a woman, gagged and bound, who watches them with eyes popping. In front of each man on the table there is a sugar cube and a pile of large bills. No one stirs. A naked bulb hangs from the ceiling by a long wire so they can see the fly count its legs. It counts them on the table, tantalizing close to a sugar cube, and then it counts them at the end of someone's nose.

I have no idea if this is the way it really was in the movie. I've worked on the scene over the years, making little adjustments in it as one does with a poem.

My life is at the mercy of my poetry.

I thought "nosology" had to do with noses. Something like a science of noses. Many noses coming to be examined. The perfect nose in the lobby of a grand hotel lighting a gold-tipped cigarette behind a potted palm. The pretty nosologist examining my nose and almost touching it with her own.

Nosology, unfortunately, has nothing to do with noses.

O beau pays! The monkey at the typewriter.

In a neighborhood frequented by muggers and rapists after dark, I bring out my soapbox and shout: "Everything I have ever said has been completely misunderstood!"

Sigmund Abeles

The first thing you notice is the skill. Abeles can draw with the best. It is not surprising that pastels are his preferred medium. They emphasize drawing, and the love of drawing is the foundation of his art.

Then there is his humanism. If Isaac Babel had been a painter this is what it would-look like. It's people that interest Abeles. There are no landscapes in his art. It's men and women in their intimate moments and dramas that he is after.

> To be in love is like going out-
> side to see what kind of day
>
> it is,

says the poet Robert Creeley in a poem called "The Business." The business of lovers, as Abeles knows well, is always to be secretly watching each other for signs of the other's inner weather. How to render that furtive look is the problem he poses himself again and again.

So, he draws, of course. As we know, no two lines drawn by hand are alike. The line is what individualizes, what gives life to the painting. Here the painter has the advantage over the poet. He can grasp the physical world in a physical way. The poet seeks the image of the world among words; the painter wears out the point of his pencil in the process of trying to get the world onto the paper.

That brings up the problem of realism. Abeles has been called a realist, as you'd expect. That doesn't mean much to

---

An introduction to an exhibition at the New England College Gallery.

me. As Paul Klee told us long ago, "Art does not reproduce the visible, but makes visible." I couldn't agree more. This is true of all authentic art. Everyone who looks at the world with the gaze of a lover makes his or her own realism. That leaves out photo-realists. They see what everybody else has already seen, and true love only sees what it wants to see. A further distinction ought to be made with the realism that keeps itself at a distance from its object. This is not Abeles's way. His art is Dionysian. He practices a passionate identification with his subject.

"Painting should be everything that theater, literature and movies often are," Abeles has said. The statement explains why he could never be an abstract painter. Silent movies and silent theater are an interesting way of thinking about his art. There are movies, for instance, from which one remembers only a single scene. Something as innocuous as a solitary figure walking by the seashore, a child at the window watching the rainy street at night, or the wide open, cloudless sky in the moment of danger. Abeles's paintings have the quality of a single frame taken out of a movie, of an image retained in memory for obscure reasons, an image that haunts us and to which we return secretly, from time to time, in order to experience anew its never-ending mystery.

"Degas kept looking when most people look away," Abeles observes in an article on the French painter, and this is true of him too. His favorite subject is a glimpse of someone's intimate moment, the one we were not meant to witness. Who has ever forgotten seeing his or her lover naked for the first time? We turned our backs, as we were told, and yet we saw what we were not supposed to see. Time stopped. The figure paused, and in that pause there was a hint of their identity and their fate. Abeles himself says: "There is a certain kind of haunting quality to a look, I guess in some way I'm trying to hold onto that."

The enigmatic Other, the abiding mystery of that which we are not, the awe and terror of that vision which the pencil and the pastel labor to make visible to us all. There's an element of transgression, voyeurism, eroticism, and even blasphemy in that. I'm thinking of Abeles's *My Lady of Mystery*, for example. Religions that have a taboo on visual representation have understood this perfectly. Art covets the Other. It blurs the distinction between the human and the divine and reveals the secret link of religious imagination to eroticism by making divinities of what is mortal and of this earth. Great art makes trouble.

This exhibition brings together some of Abeles's most significant work of the last thirty years. Rites and mini-dramas of domesticity predominate. Abeles has a small cast of characters. The titles *Sleeping Couple, The Kiss,* and *Late Night Phone Call,* give some idea of the subject matter. There are touches of humor, as in a drawing of a pair of geese, which appear to be squabbling like husband and wife. There is a magnificent *Self-Portrait on a Mirror,* which could be a parable on the ambiguity of the concept of realism. Abeles draws what he sees and what he sees is distorted, as it was for Parmigianino, who painted his reflection in a convex mirror. "Realism in this portrait no longer produces an objective truth, but a bizarria," Sidney Freedberg said of Parmigianino. I have in mind also Abeles's charcoal entitled *Folded Figure* and a number of other studies of contorted figures. These are works of stunning technical mastery and power.

I am equally fond of Abeles's portraits of old men, from the early *The Pensioner* to the the recent *The Notice* and especially *His Saturday,* in which the old guy has fallen asleep watching wrestling on TV. What affection Abeles has for these men! He doesn't sentimentalize them in the least. Here, too, there's comedy. How funny to end up looking like that, one thinks. It's what life does to us. Still, one should not insist on symbolic meaning here. It's the poetry of Abeles's images that is sufficient for me, and by poetry I mean that ability to find form and beauty in the unlikeliest of places.

Harold Rosenberg, who made sense much of the time, makes a useful point. He says: "The aim of every authentic artist is not to conform to the history of art but to release himself from it, in order to replace it with his own history." Abeles is that artist. His history—which for a painter is always the story of his Eye—is on the walls of this gallery.

Aleš Debeljak

In the beginning were the epic and the folk song. Then came the lyric poem. Someone said, "I exist," and wondered that it should be so. The world hasn't been the same since. Lyric poetry remains the place where the individual asserts himself or herself against the gods and demons of history and the tribe. In that sense the lyric poem remains potentially the most subversive of literary forms. It sings of love in time of war and prefers the loved one undressed to the sight of chariots and heroes arrayed for battle. Its secret ambition is philosophical. The lyric poem is the place where passion and metaphysics meet.

"Do you recognize yourself in this poem?" Aleš Debeljak asks. It's a question all lyric poets ask. And the answer is yes, from time to time we recognize ourselves, to our great surprise, even in a poem by a thousand-year-old Chinese poet. Memory, solitude, love, exile and return, are all there. In a lyric poem everything and everyone come together. The prose poem is the most outrageous example of this. Fable, legend, creation myth, bedtime story, travel journal, epistle, diary, dream are just some of its ingredients. The prose poem reads like a narrative but works like a lyric, since it relies on juxtaposition of images and unexpected turns of phrase. An interrupted narrative, it insists that it has to be read over and over again until its words and images radiate their full mystery. A prose poem, the way Debeljak writes it, is an invitation to the imagination; every poem is a new adventure in a new world.

Anxious Moments is an appropriate title. There are moments

Introduction to a selection of Aleš Debeljak's poems published in 1993.

of consciousness, moments of an anxious sense of our own mortality, times when we say with Debeljak: "This moment won't pass. Ever." The surprise is what comes together, things and faces, a moment that has a way of haunting our entire life from then on.

"Metaphor, yearning, the whole world," Debeljak says. Of course. In that moment of consciousness the laws of our being are to be discovered. In that sense the modern poem is epistemological. Every poem is a critical act, a phenomenology of the spirit.

Debeljak has also spoken of the influence of American poetry on his own. What American poetry offers, what may be its most attractive characteristic, is an almost total disregard for the separation of the language of prose and poetry. Even more than that, no one mixes literary and colloquial languages the way Americans do. An American poem (Pound's *Cantos* or something by Ashbery), is a quilt of various levels and types of diction. Everything is there, from latinate phrases and philosophical and scientific vocabularies to plain realistic prose and street slang. Since the main literary project everywhere and in every age is how to renew the lyric, the way the best American poetry uses all the resources of language can come in handy. That influence is more visible in Debeljak's poems in verse than in his prose poetry, but it's there, too, in the enormous freedom with which he incorporates seemingly incongruous verbal elements. What holds all this together is the emotion. All true lyric poets are exiles. This is a book of tiny odes and elegies. And they are beautiful.

The poet who is not sensitive to the enormity and complexity of our historical and intellectual predicament is not worth reading. Debeljak fulfills that difficult task "in this strange universe where one is a stranger," as Melville has said. How true that seems again! Debeljak comes from a small country that has given birth to many great poets. Edvard Kocbek and Tomaz Šalamun are perhaps the best known in the West. They too share this awe at the strangeness of our predicament.

And so the poems: a few words surrounded by much silence. My sense while reading Debeljak is that this is what pondering one's life feels like in this waning century.

Don't Squeeze the Tomatoes!

A neighbor confessed to me recently: "Maybe once or twice in my life I've tasted a truly perfect tomato." Then he proceeded to describe in lascivious detail the glories of a vine-ripened, just-picked tomato. I knew precisely what he was talking about, so I just kept nodding enthusiastically. What struck me as I listened to him is how rare and memorable the experience he was eulogizing was. Here was someone who lives in the country, who loves Italian food and buys tomatoes year round, making fussy distinctions between a ripe and a truly ripe fruit. Perfection in a tomato seems to be as elusive and to cause as much lyrical excess as romantic love. "No wonder they were called love apples by our ancestors," I said to my neighbor, and he readily agreed. There was something positively sinful about such pleasure. It would have been more appropriate if naked Eve had bitten into a beefsteak tomato, or even better, into an "Early Girl." A God who frets over his tomato plants makes more sense than the one who says, "Please don't touch my apple tree."

Thinking about apples and tomatoes I am reminded of my childhood. Every August my mother would bring baskets full of tomatoes from the country to make sauce. There'd be tomatoes in the kitchen and in every other room, tomatoes on book shelves, on tables, and even on her grand piano. Who could resist biting into them? I'd devour them the way one devours an apple. I'd take a bite, sprinkle salt on the deep red pulp, and then take another voracious bite. Of course, since the tomatoes were very ripe, the juice would run down my chin

---

This essay was published in *Antaeus* in 1994.

and onto my clothes. My mother had a brilliant solution. She'd make me strip naked and sit in the bathtub with a salt shaker and a supply of tomatoes. When I was through "making a pig of myself," in her words, I'd yell and she would come and turn the shower on and wash me off.

Biting into a ripe tomato like that is still something I love to do, although these days I remain fully dressed and only lean over the kitchen sink. One night I caught my reflection in the window above the sink. The face of a happy madman, I thought: my lips smeared, my chin and nose dripping, a half-eaten tomato in one hand, the salt shaker in the other. It's the tongue licking the lips that knows how good life can get, it occurred to me.

These memories came back to me while reading recently about a new species of super tomato being concocted by genetic engineers in California. The so-called FLVR SAVR Tomato, soon to be in your local market, is designed not to rot. Its producers claim that "it resists spoilage and can be shipped at a tasty, red-ripe stage." In short, a miracle to equal turning water into wine! The gene that causes the ordinary tomato to turn soft has been eliminated scientifically. The FLVR SAVR, one imagines, remains on the vine caressed by the golden sunlight until it reaches a perfection of ripeness. It is then harvested with maternal care and travels to your local supermarket in immaculate condition, as if it were picked minutes ago. The skin is so thin, so firm and delicate, you'll have to use your sharpest knife to slice it properly. The moment you do, that rich, fresh tomato smell will hit your nostrils. You will be in paradise. Your wife will grab a slice and you'll grab one too. "Mmmmmmmm," you'll both say together, and then you'll give each other a long sloppy kiss.

"It sounds to me like that square tomato perfect for shipping they dreamed up a few years ago," is what my wife actually said. But I wasn't dissuaded. A perfect tomato interests me in both its metaphysical and its culinary aspects. In Aristotelian terms, I believe something is perfect when it has actualized and realized its specific form. In other words, it has fulfilled its nature and found its truth. St. Thomas Aquinas sought to prove the existence of God from the degrees of perfection to be observed in the world. How close is it to divine perfection? is the question he asked. A ripe tomato out of season is a marvel. A deathless tomato is a blasphemy.

All the ramifications of this are nicely illustrated in Hawthorne's famous story "The Birth Mark." His hero Alymer, if you remember, killed his divinely beautiful spouse in the process of removing her slight imperfection, a tiny birthmark. "The pale philosopher," as Hawthorne calls him, concocted an elixir for her to drink. It worked. Briefly, he beheld her in her flawless beauty, but then his wife dropped dead. The lesson Hawthorne wants us to draw is this: it is the fatal flaw of humanity to stick its nose where it doesn't belong. Alymer, like many of us, was a philosophical idealist who denied the commonsense view that imperfection is our lot. For him the intellect was supreme, the mind was godlike, the earth could be remade into a lost Eden. He didn't make a pact with the devil in the story but he might as well have. All the smart alecks of his kind are, of course, direct descendants of Dr. Faustus. He would have understood instantly the urge to redesign the tomato in the lab.

From a culinary point of view, the temptation is perhaps even greater. I remember one viciously cold January many years ago when we discovered some fabulous Israeli tomatoes here in New Hampshire. Ordinarily, hothouse tomatoes, if that's what they were, are a huge disappointment. They look good but have no taste. These Middle Eastern tomatoes were nothing like that. They appeared in a small country store where we occasionally stopped to get gas and buy milk. Reasonably priced, tasty, ripe: it boggled the mind how they got there. Obviously someone found it profitable to fly them over that great distance. As we ate them, we imagined ancient prop planes being dragged out of junkyards to fly across the Mediterranean and the Atlantic with a load of these tomatoes. Drunks fired by major airlines, Laos and Vietnam veterans accustomed to suicide missions—how else could these tomatoes be so cheap? They were available just that one dark winter, and then, like a vision from the Arabian Nights, they vanished, never to be seen again.

The tomato craze is of a relatively recent date. I asked my

students recently if the Founding Fathers ate spaghetti with tomato sauce. Most of them were not sure, but a few said with complete confidence that they did. I ask such bizarre questions from time to time in order to test their general knowledge of history and determine how closely it has approached absolute zero. In any case, the tomato plant supposedly originated in Peru, although the word *tomatl* is Aztec, from the root *toma* meaning "to swell, grow plump," hence *toma-tl*, the plump thing. Wherever it actually came from, we know for certain that the Spainards brought it to Europe in the sixteenth-century. It was planted in Spain, Portugal, Italy, France, and England as an ornamental, but it took a couple of centuries until some unknown benefactor of future humanity actually bit into it and liked what he tasted. Mystery veils that all-important event. Like almost everything else in cookery, it must have been an accident I leave you to imagine in all its wonderful details.

For example, I read once in a medieval Byzantine book on wine making the story of how the ancient Greeks learned to make wine less alcoholic. According to the author, the wine they drank in ancient Greece was so heavy that one would get an instant hangover after one goblet. Impossible to do philosophy with such a head. All they were really capable of was putting on armor and banging each other over the head with a heavy sword. Then one day, a couple of friends were drinking wine on a terrace overlooking the sea. Suddenly it started to rain and they ran inside the house for cover, leaving their goblets outside. It was only a brief shower, so they were back on the terrace almost immediately. But when they tasted the wine they were amazed by how light, how pleasant it tasted. And that's how the Greeks learned to add water to their wine and, with suddenly cleared heads, started to ponder the nature of the universe.

As for the tomato, we are pretty sure the Italians improved it. Thomas Jefferson brought it from Europe and planted the first tomatoes on these shores in 1781, but he never ate them. An Italian painter in Salem, Massachusetts, in 1802 did that. His neighbors must have been horrified. After all, they still had not properly gotten over the witch-craft trials.

The *tomata*, as it was called and spelled then, slowly became familiar in the course of the nineteenth century. The February 1835 issue of *Harvey's American Gardener's Magazine* reported that tomatoes were being used in salads. There are preserving directions, recipes for tomato soup, and most important of all, recipes for ketchup in early nineteenth-century cook books.

Is America imaginable without ketchup? These days, even in restaurants in Europe it is not uncommon for waiters to bring a bottle of ketchup to the table, without being asked to, after realizing that their customers are American. It's surprising, therefore, to learn that until very recently there were still people in this country who believed that tomatoes were poisonous and that they might even cause cancer. The tomato plant is, of course, a relative of the deadly nightshade, so the fear has some basis.

No more. Now every market sells canned and fresh tomatoes. The greasiest spoon throws a chunk or two into the mixed salad. Of course, the difference between that tomato and the real thing is like the difference between reading about sex in a high school pamphlet and actually having it. Bred to withstand the steel fingers of the harvester, picked green, artificially reddened in ethylene gas chambers, it is chewy, sour, and flavorless and can be bounced like a ball. If there's an ideal of unsavoriness, this has to be it. No amount of zesty salad dressing, spices, or salt improves it much. We accept this poor substitute because we never stop longing for the real thing.

Gene-splicing, however, is scary. "Some 30 genetically engineered foods are waiting to be placed on the market," says the *New York Times*. We know that farmers have been crossbreeding plants since the early days of agriculture to bring out certain agreeable characteristics, but it took years to accomplish the slightest change. Genetic engineering works relatively fast. What's even more remarkable, it can combine plant genes with animal genes so, for example, a lobster can be crossbred with a tomato if one desires to make the tomato withstand cold to the degree that a lobster can.

"What if I'm allergic to lobster," says a friend of mine, "and I get the same reaction when I eat the new tomatoes?"

"It'll be like biting into a Frankenstein monster," says another deep pessimist I know.

Personally, I'm still, after three generations, a child of peasant culture. I put both elbows on the table. I break bread with my hands. I talk with my mouth full. Reading about a low-cholesterol pig "being worked on" in Princeton, New Jersey, worries me no end. How big is it gonna get if there's no fat on it at all? A colleague at the university told me about a scientist who grew a six-foot rooster by experimenting on its pituitary gland. What a crow it must have had! I hear it was slow and awkward, and ended up being killed by a mutt who did not care for its looks.

If my father were alive today he too would have been attracted and repelled by the promise of this new tomato. In his view, which I share completely, a salad of ripe tomatoes is one of the glories of life. First of all, it smells good. There are onions in it, hot green peppers, basil, and olive oil. It's a simple dish, but to do it properly the proportions have to be just right. Too much of this, too little of that, and it's not quite the same thing. This is an art of nuance in which the senses of taste and smell reign supreme. Generalizations and abstractions in the form of recipes and measuring cups and spoons have no place here. The tongue is more subtle than the word. Like the poets, it doesn't believe in a single meaning. Stick your face in the bowl, my father advised.

To do complete justice to such a salad one must have a loaf of coarse Italian or French bread on the side. The bread makes the wine taste better and is needed at the end to wipe the bowl clean. That wonderful mixture of oil, onion, herb, and tomato juice beats any elixir Alymer and his kind can come up with.

My wife objects. She prefers the more elegant French way of making the salad in which the tomato is not sliced into chunks but into thin slices, which are then laid on the plate and sprinkled with freshly made vinaigrette. I remember once being told in a small neighborhood restaurant in Paris that tomatoes in vinaigrette was the only thing they had in the way of an appetizer. I was disappointed, but not after I tasted what they brought me. There were only four slices on the plate and they were exquisitely flavored. I sipped a light rosé and wiped the plate with bread under the approving gaze of the fat proprietor.

The moment the subject of good tomatoes comes up, memory starts its parade: Jersey tomatoes sold on the streets of New York, roadside stands in New England and California. Late summer feasts in backyards and restaurants with a garden. Tomatoes posing alone. Tomatoes with anchovies, with tuna, with sliced cucumbers, with black olives, with young mozzarella, with poached fish, with capers, with potatoes, with eggplant, with sausages. Tomatoes in various pasta sauces. All the Provençal, Greek, Sicilian, and Spanish casseroles. Hearty minestrones. Pots of steaming bouillabaisse and other Mediterranean fish stews. Cold gazpachos with bottles of well-chilled white wine.

Cucina e Nostalgiá is the title of a gastronomic memoir by a master Italian chef, Alfredo Viazzi, which was published some years ago. That describes the way we all talk about food. In every inspired conversation about a meal, there is a longing to savor once again that delicious last drop, that piquant morsel of some gorgeously prepared dish and bring back that long ago day when we were truly happy in the company of a few friends or a lover.

"Nostalgia is now," the producers of the FLVR SAVR should have shouted from the rooftops! Instead, they said: "The data demonstrate that the FLVR SAVR tomato is as safe and nutritious as the currently available fresh tomatoes." Not everybody was convinced. A certain Mr. Jeremy Rifkin has recently formed a group called the Pure Food Campaign, which has declared war on the FLVR SAVR. Environmental groups are understandably concerned about the potential consequences of altering the biological makeup of foods by cell-cloning or moving genes from animals into plants. Reuters reported last October that "1000 US chefs have announced that they'll boycott bioengineered food." A thousand chefs all wearing chefs' hats and shaking their wooden spoons at us is nothing to take lightly.

"I will not sacrifice the entire history of culinary art to revitalize the biotechnology industry," declared Rick Monner, executive chef at the Water Club Restaurant. Yes, of course, but then there's Rebecca Goldburg, a senior scientist with the Environmental Defense Fund, who said that unlike Rifkin, her group is not opposed to all genetically engineered foods.

I'm as wary of scientists in the kitchen as my grandmother was of men, but what if this tomato is harmless and simply tastes great? There's genetically engineered Florida corn, which my greengrocer tells me is already on the market and doesn't taste bad. Also, what if foods can be made more nutritious and the need for nasty pesticides and chemical fertilizers eliminated at the same time?

Being of two minds, I figured, why not conduct a quick poll of my own, have my own private *Donahue* show with a few friends and neighbors whose taste buds and good sense I trust?

What I heard is not exactly what I expected. Here's a sampling of their views:

"I put cow shit on my tomatoes and it doesn't prevent me from eating them."

"It's hard to believe they didn't have tomatoes in Roman orgies."

"Just another product of a body-builder mentality."

"Tomato juice is the best cure for hangovers."

"It's the rot in the fruit that makes it taste good. You can't get rid of one without getting rid of the other.

"Be sure to see *Attack of the Killer Tomatoes.*"

"I'd like to know when was the first rotten tomato thrown at a performer?"

"The sad truth is that we Americans have forgotten that even a tomato has a soul."

"I remember a chicken that told fortunes," somebody's mother said, to which the rest of us shouted, "What the hell does that have to do with tomatoes?"

UNDER DISCUSSION
Donald Hall, General Editor

Volumes in the Under Discussion series collect reviews and essays about individual poets. The series is concerned with contemporary American and English poets about whom the consensus has not yet been formed and the final vote has not been taken. Titles in the series include:

Elizabeth Bishop and Her Art
  edited by Lloyd Schwartz and Sybil P. Estess
Richard Wilbur's Creation
  edited and with an Introduction by Wendy Salinger
Reading Adrienne Rich
  edited by Jane Roberta Cooper
On the Poetry of Allen Ginsberg
  edited by Lewis Hyde
Robert Bly: When Sleepers Awake
  edited by Joyce Peseroff
Robert Creeley's Life and Work
  edited by John Wilson
On the Poetry of Galway Kinnell
  edited by Howard Nelson
On Louis Simpson
  edited by Hank Lazer
Anne Sexton
  edited by Steven E. Colburn
James Wright
  edited by Peter Stitt and Frank Graziano
Frank O'Hara
  edited by Jim Elledge
On the Poetry of Philip Levine
  edited by Christopher Buckley
The Poetry of W. D. Snodgrass
  edited by Stephen Haven
Denise Levertov
  edited with an introduction by Albert Gelpi
On William Stafford
  edited by Tom Andrews

A forthcoming volume will examine the work of Gwendolyn Brooks. *Please write for further information on available editions and current prices.*

Ann Arbor

The University of Michigan Press